PRAISE FOR
SELL IT NOW, SELL IT TODAY

"Hopkins is a dynamic, ethically sound sales trainer with a rich background of personal and business success. His methods and techniques are practical, field tested, and effective."

~ Zig Ziglar, legendary motivational speaker, New York Times Bestselling Author of *Secrets of Closing the Sale*

"Tom Hopkins is head and shoulders above the rest when it comes to training high-powered sales professionals."

**~ Harvey Mackay,
New York Times Bestselling Author of
*Swim with the Sharks Without Being Eaten Alive***

"Three weeks into studying Mr. Hopkins' materials my sales went 'through the roof'. Tom's teachings have allowed me to be of service to countless numbers of people throughout the years."

**~ Bob Burg, professional speaker,
National Bestselling Author of *Endless Referrals***

SELL IT TODAY, SELL IT NOW

SELL IT TODAY, SELL IT NOW

Mastering the Art of the One-Call Close

Tom Hopkins

Pat Leiby

Made for Success
PUBLISHING

Made For Success Publishing
P.O. Box 1775 Issaquah, WA 98027
www.MadeForSuccessPublishing.com

Distributed by Made For Success Publishing

Second Printing

Library of Congress Cataloging-in-Publication data
Hopkins, Tom
Leiby, Pat
    Sell it Today, Sell it Now: Mastering the Art of the One-Call Close
    p. cm.
        ISBN: 9781613398517
        LCCN: 2015915799

Printed in the United States of America

Published in partnership with by Tom Hopkins International, Inc.
465 East Chilton Drive, Suite 4
Chandler, Arizona USA 85225
480.949.0786
800.528.0446
www.tomhopkins.com
info@tomhopkins.com

About the Authors

Tom Hopkins is world-renowned as America's #1 sales trainer. Since 1976, he has helped millions of sales professionals around the world serve more people through the use of proven-effective communication and sales skills. His simple, yet persuasive, how-to strategies have increased the incomes of salespeople and companies alike.

Tom wasn't always successful. His first 90 dzays in sales, he earned only $150. However, through self-education and persistence, he soon learned that selling was a skill like any other that could be honed and fine-tuned. He went on to set records in real estate sales that remained unbroken for decades.

His public seminars sell out and his customized, private programs receive rave reviews. Tom's books have sold in the millions and hundreds of thousands of people benefit from his online courses and recorded audio and video programs every day

Pat Lieby - After graduating from high school and spending seven years lying on basement floors working on greasy washing machines as an appliance mechanic, Pat Leiby decided there must be a better way. Remembering the friendly debit insurance salesman that called at the Leiby home, Pat got a job with the same company in a poor neighborhood in Akron, Ohio. Pat quickly became hooked on sales, but debit accounting was not his forté.

For the next several years, Pat developed his own personal skills and a system of selling, which turned out to be a blessing in disguise. By applying his proprietary system, which is the basis for the strategies within these pages, Pat increased one company's sales volume by 500% and was the number one salesperson in various other companies. Pat also designed sales presentations and trained timeshare sales professionals who did over $2 billion in sales volume with his system.

Note: Sadly, Pat Leiby passed away in 2014. Tom Hopkins International, Inc. is proud to keep his legacy alive by continuing to publish this book.

Dedication

To true sales professionals around the globe,
who are my inspiration in everything I do.

Tom Hopkins

To my wife, Janie, for her advice, encouragement,
and support in this effort and many others.

Pat Leiby

Tom Hopkins'
Acknowledgements

Words cannot express my gratitude to Pat Leiby. In him, I found a phenomenal resource and vast well of knowledge in the area of the one-call close.

I also acknowledge Dan Baldwin, one of our writers, who is a joy to work with. Thank you for tearing our notes apart and putting them back together in an easy-to-read manner. Your talent for clarifying points and creating analogies make this book a great tool for our readers.

To Judy Slack who has managed my content for nearly 40 years. Thank you for pulling all the pieces together to make this book come true.

Pat Leiby's Acknowledgements

To Tom Hopkins, whom I consider the world's greatest sales trainer, for giving me the opportunity to collaborate with him. I am grateful and flattered.

David Siegel, for his inspiration by being the epitome of the American Dream.

Jim Gissy, one of the most all-around successful men I've ever met, for his constant help and support.

Bill Hall and Carole Gehan, friends and former students, for keeping me on track and supplying helpful input.

Gene Lloyd, one of my early trainers and confidantes.

Norma Rivera, who spent countless hours trying to read my handwriting.

Finally, all of my mentors over the years, too numerous to mention, who guided, taught, pushed, and shoved me through my life and sales success.

I thank you.

Table of Contents

Introduction

A true professional, a real champion in sales, is constantly working toward closing. Most salespeople, especially the folks in retail, may have one and only one opportunity to serve the needs of any given customer. Others, those people in high-dollar markets for example, will invest a lot more time and energy to make a sale. Still, the entire process, no matter how brief or how drawn out, comes down to a one-time opportunity to close.

That's what this book is all about—the art of one-call closing. We also refer to the process as one-*time* closing and both terms are used interchangeably throughout this book.

We have invested decades into studying, learning, practicing and perfecting one-call closing techniques. We have discovered a profoundly simple, yet profoundly effective process for it. It's not magic. It's not manipulation. It's just a very logical way to match your product or service to the specific needs of your buyer in a one-time closing situation. In the following pages, we will show you specifically how to combine your people skills and your basic sales techniques into this powerful sales strategy.

It works. We have tried it, tested it, taught it, improved it and now, best of all, we're sharing it. Think of the one-call closing process as one of those ancient circular mazes where the traveler starts on the outside and eventually winds his or her way to the center. That's what you'll be doing. Every step in the process brings you closer to your ultimate goal—serving the needs of your buyer. Every move helps you zero in closer and closer until you are finally home at the win/win situation of a successful close.

Creating the Right Place
at the Right Time

We predict that in the pages of this book you will be amazed to discover a number of time-tested and proven ideas that will work for you. We have combined proven, powerful ideas with other, more familiar techniques that we have each taught over the years. The result is a dynamic, step-by-step manual for those people fortunate enough to be earning a living in sales.

Sell It Today, Sell It Now™, Mastering the Art of the One-Call Close will show the newcomer and the veteran alike how to develop champion sales presentations for any sales situation by using the correct sequence for every potential buyer.

You've no doubt heard the phrases, *"timing is ninety percent of genius"* and *"he was in the right place at the right time."* Using the techniques in this book will show you how to say the right words at the right time. In other words, you'll learn how to create the right sequence for maximum effect.

There are no new words in sales. We all draw from the same pool of words, phrases, and expressions and the pool isn't any deeper for top closers than it is for those on the bottom rungs of the ladder to success. Why, then is there such a disparity between top salespeople and the also-rans? The difference is that the top closer's presentations are in harmony with the mindsets of their buyers. Their presentations are in the proper sequence. In many cases, the top pros have developed and refined their presentations after years of experience and trial and error. The process in this book will shorten your learning curve exponentially, helping you to refine your presentation in a matter of days.

In later pages, we provide examples of how the sequence of events can and does affect all aspects of our lives. For the moment, the proper sequence for you is to read this book and put into action the techniques and methods contained in these pages.

Speaking of later pages, throughout this book we use a number of examples and scenarios featuring a variety of products and services. Naturally, we have chosen some of the most prominent so that the examples apply to the broadest possible audience.

But please remember, the principles, techniques, strategies, and tactics you find here will apply across the board. Whether you're offering insurance or interior design, financial services or corporate planes, home improvements or highways, real estate or real-time streaming video, this book is for you.

Your goal is to present your product or service in such a way that the only sensible choice is for your potential client to make a buying decision and to make it right now.

The Art of One-Call Closing is More Than a One-Time Read

An associate in the advertising profession told us about the absolute necessity of repetition in selling. He says that numerous studies dating back at least to the early 1960s prove that consumers don't even recognize that they've read/viewed/listened to an ad, TV commercial, or radio spot (or whatever medium) until they've been exposed to it six times. And that's just *recognition*. The selling hasn't even begun at that point.

We also remember an important lesson a speed-reading instructor taught us. The purpose of speed-reading isn't to get through the written word faster. The purpose is to be able to get through the book several times in the same time period. The more you read the same material, the more you retain and will be able to put to good use.

We don't want this book to be a one-time read for the very same reason. The more you study this book, the more you will get out of it, and the more it will enrich your life and enhance your future.

We recommend that you read it once straight through and then go back through it again. Keep it nearby so you can refer to it often as you plan your presentations. It is our hope and our belief that you will find it a constant, positive source of

information, thought-provoking ideas, and inspiration.

CHAPTER 1

*Timing is everything. It is as important
to know* when *as to know* how.

~Arnold Glasow

The One-Time Job Description

Most retail sales are one-time closes, or should be. The customer walks in, you make an approach, a presentation and then an effective close. You follow that up with: *"Thank you so much, and please visit us again."* But even when helping people get involved with high-dollar items requiring multiple consultations, there's a distant-but-inevitable moment when the planets are in alignment, the stars are in your favor, and it's time for a close. That's the moment for a one-time close, as well. It's a one-time *opportunity.*

Regardless of your sales experience, or the lack of it, you are about to embark on a brand new leg of your career focused on the art of the one-time close. No matter how many years you have in the business, no matter how much real-world experience you've racked up, and apart from those *"Salesperson of the Month"* plaques you've earned, when you adopt the principles in **Sell It Today, Sell It Now™, Mastering the Art of the One-Call Close**, it's as if you are starting a new job.

The one-call close approach is so different from what you've likely already mastered that it requires different thinking about what your job as a salesperson is all about. And, the benefit you will gain is a greater closing ratio … and a bigger paycheck.

Why are people in sales? What is the job description of someone required to close sales on the first and only opportunity? We've asked this question in classes and seminars all around the country.

Some of the more popular answers are:

- to sell a product

- to feed my family

- to serve the needs of others

- to identify the needs of another person

- to show a product to a prospect

- to explain the benefits of a product or service

- to make enough money to _____

Certainly, these are valid reasons, but they're not very accurate. That's like describing your reason for taking a passenger jet is because you like the peanuts, the in-flight movie, or you just have a thing for turbulence. All of those reasons may be valid, but that's not why you purchased your ticket. The real answer for why we do what we do eludes most people, even those who have for years reaped the benefits of this most wonderful of professions.

What sets the one-call close salesperson apart from the rest? Most of the products, services, and ideas we offer provide genuine benefits to our customers just like the rest of the world's salespeople. We all help people get where they want to go. For most salespeople, the presentation is centered on features, turning those features into benefits and then offering proof to back up their statements. That is well and good and certainly necessary. After all, we wouldn't be as happy on that cross-country trip without those peanuts and in-flight movies.

However, you don't have to be a rocket scientist to know that the focus of a one-time closer is not on the peanuts or the movie, but like a laser beam, it is on selling *today* and selling *now*. And believe us, this is an art form, but it is an art form that you can learn, apply, and even improve your skills with by internalizing the techniques in this book.

The difference in the art of the one-time close is in the significant amount of planning, time, and energy the salesperson invests in the process of closing sales. Therefore, the job description of the one-time closing salesperson is someone who can sell it today, sell it now!

Tom says: *You achieve success in sales when you (1) find the people to sell to, and (2) sell to the people you find.*

Pat says: *Especially when you do it right now.*

Using the Full-Court Press

We have created this book for two types of salespeople:

1. Those whose jobs are defined by a need for the one-time close.

2. Those whose jobs evolve into a one-time closing situation.

In other words, this book is for everyone in sales. Despite our intense focus on closing, we do not advocate, nor do we recommend using high-pressure sales techniques. Ever! And we haven't just served you up a big, heaping helping of contradiction either.

25

The age of the high-pressure salesperson has gone the way of the dinosaur. It is as extinct as those T-Rex bones archeologists keep digging up[1].

Our techniques focus on continual, gentle persuasion targeted to getting a one-time close without using high-pressure techniques. We can help you overcome a customer's natural indecision and reluctance to autograph your paperwork.

One of the worst experiences a salesperson can have is to make a heartfelt, enthusiastic, and sincere presentation only to hear:

- *"I'd like to think about it some more."*

- *"Well, thanks. I'll have to get back to you."*

- *"You've given me a lot to think about."*

- *"That's certainly food for thought."*

- *"Could I have your card before I go?"*

- *"We don't jump in to something like this."*

The full court press is a basketball term in which the defensive team doesn't run to the offense's end of the court to get in to position and then wait for the other team to show up with the ball. They start playing defense immediately at their end of the court, forcing the team with the ball to fight for every inch of the floor.

The one-time closing master works for the close every second of their presentation. From the first second of *"Hello,*

---

1   *We understand from the folks in Hollywood that the age of the dinosaur, at least the computer-generated kind, has returned. That may be true, but salespeople today don't live in a cartoon world. No matter how animated the presentation, the high-pressure salesperson is likely to end up in some future museum with the other dinosaurs where incredulous people walk around thinking, "I wonder how they ever managed to live like that?"

what brings you folks out here today" to the *"just authorize here to arrange for installation,"* the salesperson is building toward the inevitable, successful close. It really is a full-court press designed to make sure your buyer gets the benefits of the goods and services she or he wants, needs and are truly good for them.

"I sold my heart out, but I just couldn't close him." How often have you heard that? How often have you said it?

The one-call close puts the focus of the sales presentation where it belongs—on the close, which is the natural progression of selling. We do that by creating a genuine and honest sense of urgency throughout the presentation. It's a full-court press designed to help your buyer get the one, unique product or service (yours) that perfectly matches his or her unique need.

Someday Selling

The problem many salespeople have is what we call *"someday selling."* They don't have a plan or system to close a sale now; instead, they're working toward some ill-defined point in the future. That future *"someday"* may be only minutes down the road, but without the skills and techniques in this book, that someday might remain in the future. You may have heard the saying, "Someday never comes."

What makes someday selling worse is that the salesperson understands what's happening too late to do anything about it. Feeling desperate, he or she will start using high-pressure sales techniques (not one-time closing) to resurrect this sales opportunity. The customer notices the change in tactics, gets suspicious, and ends up going across the street where the salespeople aren't perceived as being so pushy.

We often hear that it takes pressure to create a diamond. Rarely do we hear the other side of that story. A diamond isn't created by abrupt pressure. It's created by continual, well-directed pressure over time. Do you see the difference? More important, your potential new client will feel the difference.

Use Outside Factors to Get the Inside Track

Our one-call close shows you how to create a proper sense of urgency throughout your presentation which will lead directly to the win/win situation of a successful close today.

External factors can be used effectively to create the necessary urgency for your buyer to make a decision sooner rather than later. Again, we're not saying you should use or create a false sense of urgency. Not only is that dishonest. It's unnecessary. There are always plenty of legitimate external factors at your fingertips.

For example:

"This is the last SUV on the lot with this option package."

"With our stock of winter coats being on sale, by tomorrow morning, I expect this entire rack to be empty."

"We're selling an average of three houses a week in this development. We only have three lots left, and only one with the north-facing exposure you want."

"Four of my clients from last week have already come back to order more of these."

"We are reducing our inventory to make room for new models, so we're offering some really great special investments on our current inventory through the end of the month."

"I understand that the company is discontinuing the line next year. These are the last ones ever."

All of these examples are justifiable uses of urgency to legitimately serve a customer's need. In later chapters, we will describe in detail all the skills and knowledge you need to create this sense of urgency so you can close sales in just one call.

One-Time Closing by Degrees

The illustration below uses a thermometer to show how a typical buyer feels at the beginning of the sales process. This is a before sketch which will be followed by *"during"* and *"after" sketches as the book progresses.* As if you didn't already know, the potential client usually meets you with a fairly high degree of sales resistance. In fact, he (or she) could be near the boiling point of resistance at 100 degrees.

Decrease Sales Resistance Chart "Before" Phase

Wait, you say. If the buyer has logged on, made a call, or walked in to your store that shows at least some level of acceptance, doesn't it? The answer is yes ... and no. Yes, the customer is interested in the product or service. That doesn't mean he's interested a bit in your specific brand, your company, or the various models and options you offer. The degree of resistance you face at that initial moment of contact is right up there, pegging out at or near 100 degrees. Don't ever assume otherwise.

Any pressure applied at this point will raise that level of resistance even higher. The situation could easily bubble over the top and you'll never get the opportunity to present, much less close a sale.

Your first job is to begin rapidly lowering the buyer's temperature. If you give your buyer half a chance, he or she will help you do it. Remember, deep down inside they really want the benefits of your product or service or they wouldn't have made or agreed to the contact. Again, if you apply undue or sudden pressure, your buyers will seek relief elsewhere. They may bubble over, head out the nearest exit, cross the street and enter a more comfortable zone at your competitor's operation.

Buyers don't visit your show room, call your 800 number, or spend time on your web site in order to feel uncomfortable. See to it that they feel relaxed, comfortable, and right at home immediately by lowering that temperature as quickly as possible. No one invests their money in anything unless they are relaxed and comfortable.

The next chart illustrates what (ideally) should be happening during the various stages of your presentation.

Slowly but surely, degree by degree, the buyer's sales resistance is reduced. People buy from people they like and trust. The more you build rapport and trust, the more willing they will be to make that purchase. You can't really start the sales process in earnest until you reduce sales resistance.

But, as they say on infomercials and television game shows, *"Wait! There's more!"*

Look back at the *"during"* chart and notice that as you reduce sales resistance, you are, in effect creating an empty space—a vacuum—and nature abhors a vacuum. Hypnotherapists recognize this factor and wisely incorporate it into their programs.

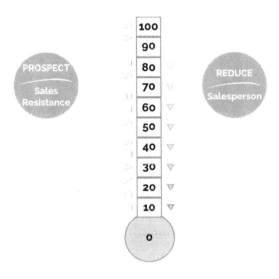

Decrease Sales Resistance Chart "During" Phase

For example, if a therapist cures an overeater by removing the craving for chocolate bonbons, a vacuum is created. Whatever motivated the client to overeat is gone, but there's a huge hole in the client's life. (Yes, and belly, too.) Something will rush in to fill that vacuum. One of those "something's" could be the client's old bonbon habit or a new ice cream or potato chip habit. That's why the hypnotherapists fill the void with another, more positive behavior such as drinking water or chewing gum.

As salespeople, we have to do exactly the same thing. When we remove sales resistance, we have to fill that vacuum we've created with something positive, such as enticing information on the benefits of owning our products. Otherwise, resistance could easily slip back in.

31

Practice a little sales therapy and replace those negatives with positives. And those positives will lead to ... sales acceptance.

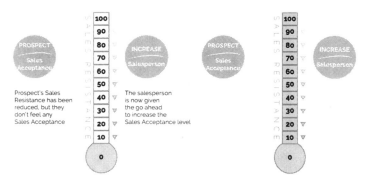

Increase Sales Acceptance Chart "During" Phase   **Increase Sales Acceptance Chart "After" Phase**

Replace Sales Resistance with Sales Acceptance

Notice the difference between the *"before"* and the *"after"* charts above. You convert 100 degrees of negative into 100 degrees of positive. Sales resistance is completely replaced with sales acceptance as you zero in on the heart of that maze we mentioned earlier. Degree by degree you increase the sales acceptance temperature until you have reached a favorable climate for a win/win sales opportunity. And you don't have to use high pressure to do it.

As we indicated earlier, nature will not tolerate a vacuum. The next time you see a news report about a drought somewhere on planet Earth, notice that there will be floods in another part of the globe. When it's unusually cold in one hemisphere, you will find that it is unusually hot in another. Nature balances out and the game of sales is where you get to play Mother Nature. Keep your buyers well-balanced by filling all that empty space you create by reducing sales resistance with sales acceptance so they have a desire to say *"yes"* to your product now.

This slow-but-steady, soft approach may seem foreign to you if you're used to a more "hard charger" approach, but this approach works phenomenally well. We and the hundreds of thousands of people who have studied our principles, prove it year after year, decade after decade.

Your Buyer is His/Her Own Worst Enemy

The sales game is sometimes like a baseball game with the salesperson as the pitcher and the buyer swinging the bat. You keep pitching your best stuff, but he keeps hitting them out of the park.

By the way, this analogy is where the term *"pitch"* came from in selling many years ago. It is a word we strongly recommend you remove from your vocabulary unless you're talking about baseball. While you're at it, remove the image of tossing anything at your potential client and move on to a smarter way of winning the game.

For example, let's suppose you're about to settle in for an evening with your family, a good book, or some great music. Suddenly, the phone rings and Mr. Hy Pressure starts his pre-planned, pre-programmed, pre-industrial presentation on investing in mutual funds. Instead of listening to your favorite tunes you're hearing a string of verbal nonsense about compound interest, steady returns, and modest investments. Naturally, you offer a polite thanks-but-no-thanks, hang up and get back to your evening plans. It is safe to say that your sales resistance is at 100 degrees.

Later, however, you could be surfing the web and you venture across the website of the company that Hy Pressure represents. You're about to click away when a sentence captures your attention. *"Want To Earn Steady Returns With Modest In-*

vestment? Click Here." You click and are redirected immediately to a fact-filled page about the joys of mutual fund investing. Sounds interesting, you think.

You notice another eye-catching phrase. *"Want To Learn More About The Magic Of Compound Interest? Click Here."* Again, you click and again you're taken to another page where you learn how one dollar can become two and how two can become four, eight, sixteen and you can earn real wealth before you retire. Now, you're intrigued. You also notice that there's a free telephone consultation available. The site even offers a toll-free telephone number. You dial. You reach Ms. O.T. Close. You ask questions, get answers, and half an hour later you find your sales resistance has been lowered to almost zero. You're starting to get excited about the benefits of investing.

But you still don't own those mutual funds. Why? Your sales resistance has not yet been replaced with sales acceptance. The negative space needs to be filled with positive content.

Fortunately, Ms. Close is a master salesperson and is about to bring you to the point where you are prepared to open an account with her company.

It's important to note that building sales acceptance is a process. It's something you do by degrees—step by step.

We've heard the theory that there are no true opposites in the universe. For example, at what point does black become white? At what temperature does cold become hot? At what decibel does quiet become loud? Instead of clearly defined lines, the universe is made up of degrees of change.

Black and white are merely two ends of the same spectrum separated by degrees of change. Changing sales resistance to sales acceptance is the same. Degree by degree we help our buyer make that transition. *"No sale"* soon becomes *"sold."*

Let's return to that toll-free call with Ms. O.T. Close. She says that since you are working directly with the company, there are no middle-men involved. She is in a position to offer the same mutual funds, stocks or bonds other companies offer, but at a discounted fee.

Your interest is piqued. *"Tell me more,"* you say. And she does. She can also offer the company's $57 *"Guide To Investing In The New Age"* absolutely free, but only while supplies last. Sold! A minute or so later you have made a commitment to open an account and are on your way to earning steady returns on your modest investment via the magic of compound interest.

We have taught people this sales process throughout the world. It's worked millions of times and will work millions of times more. By first reducing sales resistance and then gaining sales acceptance, master salespeople have helped millions of people acquire cars and houses, boats and planes, businesses, investments, educations, and comfortable futures. And most of those satisfied buyers began the process at or near 100 degrees of sales resistance.

Such is the *"magic"* of a well-trained salesperson.

It's Two Jobs, Two Jobs, Two Jobs in One!

Many years ago Certs breath mints ran a famous advertising campaign featuring pairs of twins as their friendly, smiling, fresh-breathed spokespersons. The angle of the ads was to increase market share by promoting a breath mint as a candy mint, too. One twin would claim *"Certs is a breath mint."* The other would say *"Certs is a candy mint"* and then the announcer would prove them both right with *"It's two mints, two mints, two mints in one!"*

The art of the one-time close is actually two jobs, two jobs, two jobs in one:

Job One is to reduce sales resistance.

Job Two is to gain sales acceptance.

You must complete Job One before you can effectively begin Job Two. You can't mix them up or you'll mess up your chances of success.

The process is quite simple. That doesn't mean it is easy. This is compounded by the fact that most salespeople are good at one job and not quite so proficient at the other. A person who is really good at making friends and disarming buyers may be nervous and tentative at closing and asking for the money or an endorsement of the agreement.

Conversely, the good closer can be overly eager in the initial stages of the process. *"Hi, I'm Bob. Sign this."* He or she risks losing the sale before even getting a good start. That is where our turning Sales Resistance into Sales Acceptance system comes into play.

CHAPTER 2

The Salesperson's Mind

The English politician and statesman, Lord Chesterfield, compared a weak mind to a microscope, always magnifying the tiniest things out of proportion while missing the big picture. There's a lot of truth there, especially for people building careers in sales. We salespeople must prepare our minds to be strong, flexible, and always ready to accept the latest challenge.

Now that we have covered your job description, let's get on with preparing you to handle that job to your best ability. Let's start preparing your mind to embrace the big picture.

If you don't already have an open mind, now is the time to bring out your mental can opener. Take a lesson from Chapter One. As we lower your resistance to learning a new system for closing the sale, we'll be increasing your acceptance of the one-time closing strategy. We'll create a negative space by helping you wash your mind clear of outdated ideas and replace that empty space with exciting new ones.

Fear is the salesperson's greatest obstacle and showing you how to eliminate it is the chief goal of this chapter. A champion one-time closer recognizes fear for what it is, handles it and moves ahead with the task of serving the buyer's needs. Let's take a closer look at fear. C'mon, what are you afraid of?

Fear. Son of Fear. Fear's Revenge.

Even the most knowledgeable and most experienced of us face fear on a regular basis, even daily. Taking on the challenge of a sales career naturally puts you in situations which can bring up certain anxieties. Sometimes these fears are tiny little things gnawing at our confidence. Other times they're like an army of Vandals stampeding over the gates about to ransack and pillage our homes. How you handle those natural fears will, to a great extent, determine your success in sales.

So, what are our most common fears?

They are:

- Fear of loss

- Fear of the past

- Fear of the unknown

- Fear of failure

- Fear of the future

- Fear of making a mistake

That covers a lot of ground, doesn't it? We're pretty sure you'll find a bit of yourself somewhere in that list. And that's okay. Truth be told, a little bit of all of us is in there. Yes, even your authors get the jitters now and then.

Fear of loss often paralyzes salespeople. So much so that they actually create the thing they fear most—loss of sales. Champion salespeople realize that they will inevitably lose some sales. And that's okay. It's just part of the process. They accept it and move on.

As they say in basketball, *"you can't score if you don't shoot."* In the long run, the misses don't matter as much as you might think because they're more than balanced by what you learn from them. That knowledge leads to the shots that go through the hoops. In other words, don't let your fear of loss create loss.

Fear of the past isn't a reference to reincarnation and your unfortunate encounter with those hungry lions back when you were a rather clumsy Roman gladiator. We're talking about a more recent past, perhaps as recent as yesterday or even this morning.

We all make mistakes that we are fearful of repeating. Have you ever gone into a presentation unprepared or lacking in commitment? You bombed, didn't you? The fear of repeating a past mistake can be hard to handle because you've had actual experience with the pain it causes. And now, justifiably so, you're afraid of a repeat performance. Who wouldn't be? It hurts!

Fear of the unknown is just the opposite. In approaching a sale, you're scared of something of which you have no experience or point of reference. In some ways, it's worse than some of the other fears because your mind can create all kinds of scenarios that are much, much scarier than whatever-the-heck the real thing may be.

The average salesperson thinks, *"I don't know what I'm about to experience, therefore it scares me out of my mind."* For top salespeople, the unknown isn't something to be feared, rather something to be embraced. Their curiosity about the unknown overpowers their fear. The unknown should be thought of as a learning experience and after all, that's where you find success.

Fear of failure is a natural byproduct of wanting to take action. *"Since I haven't a clue as to what is about to happen, I'm afraid I'll fail."* Of course, nobody can be sure that he or she is 100% prepared for the next challenge. Even the most prepared salesperson faces the possibility that the buyer may toss them a fast curve ball.

The unexpected is a constant threat to any sales presentation. The important thing is to remember that failure leads to success for those willing to learn from their presentation mistakes. Think of failure as a tool. It's not something to be avoided.

In fact, you can't avoid it 100% of the time unless you never meet a new potential client, which would put you out of the sales business, wouldn't it? So, study your mistakes. Learn from your failures and create a new inevitable ... inevitable success.

Fear of the future is the negative side of your mind (we all have one) saying, *"Whoa! Slow down there. You're getting ahead of yourself."* Even top salespeople who have achieved remarkable levels of success face this challenge. *"Will I be able to do this again? Can I sustain my momentum? What if I drop the ball?"*

The future, by definition, is unknown and if we allow the negative side of our minds to take over, we can create a frighteningly bleak future. Like the country/western comedy song from the old television program, *"Hee Haw," we see nothing but "doom, despair, and agony on me, deep dark depression, excessive misery."*

Look at it this way, most people in the work force don't have near the opportunity for building a future as bright as we lucky folks in sales. Your future is an exciting event that you can shape with your own hands. Surely, that's something to create excitement rather than fear.

Fear of making a mistake often arises from thoughts about past mistakes, earlier presentations that just didn't pan out as expected. As you get into a discussion of the exchange of their money for your product or service, there's this fear that it could happen again.

As with fear of loss and failure, the fear of making a mistake is a misguided one. Of course, you're going to make a mistake—probably way more than one. We all have. We all will. And, that's okay. Just learn from them. Perfect your presentation and keep your potential client's best interests at heart, and you'll be amazed at how many fewer mistakes you make than someone who doesn't do it this way. Part of your presentation has to reinforce the correctness and the intelligence of the purchase—that taking ownership of the product or service now, today, is a wise decision.

Face Facts and Freeze-Out Fear

Fear can be *de*structive or *con*structive. The outcome all depends upon how and how well you handle it. Or, how you let it handle you! All of these fears can be controlled and, in some cases, even put to good use. Once you understand how fear affects you personally, you will begin to see how it creates obstacles between you and your goals. These obstacles—even when they're only *perceived* and not real—can create significant challenges. They can cause you to lose a sale, a job, a client, and even a career. Does it really matter that there's not a hungry lion behind the door, if your fear of becoming tonight's supper keeps you from stepping through it?

Once you use the strategies in this book, fear will begin to fade. Sometimes it will fade away to nothingness. Even if it does stick around for a while, you'll be able to control it.

Some people actually use their fears to spur them on. As one salesperson said, "*I am more afraid of not bringing home a paycheck to my wife and kids than I am of the buyer saying no to me, the person on the other end of the line hanging up on me, or even the world-famous CEO behind the mahogany desk.*"

Tom says: *Never seek career advice from your fears.*

Pat says: *Being scared of something that has not yet happened is like crying over spilled milk that hasn't yet spilled! What purpose does it serve?*

41

When Knowledge Comes in the Door, Fear Jumps Out the Window

The six fears just named are usually grounded in the salesperson's perception of their own level of competency—in how well the individual thinks he or she performs at the job. As we increase our levels of knowledge, we automatically see increases in competence.

This brings us back to our thermometer illustration from the previous chapter. As knowledge helps you drop your fear from the 100-degree level, that vacuum is replaced by a positive force known as competence.

We have studied the subject in-depth, and understand that there are four basic levels of competence. These levels especially apply when you are learning anything new—such as tying your shoes, learning computer skills, or mastering one-time closing. These are:

- Level #1—The Unconscious Incompetent

- Level #2—The Conscious Incompetent

- Level #3—The Conscious Competent

- Level #4—The Unconscious Competent

Different authors and lecturers may use different terminology, but the basis remains the same. Let's see how this relates to salespeople. Specifically, let's see how all this relates to you.

Level #1. The *unconscious incompetent* doesn't even know that he (or she) doesn't know what he's doing. Like the kid trying to make his first bow in the laces of his tennis shoes, or the CEO learning her first computer program, we experience Level #1 all our lives. Or, at least as long as we keep trying new things.

In that sense, unconscious incompetence is a necessary evil. Generally, there's nothing to be embarrassed about. If you take up rollerblading as part of your new exercise program, you can count on being an unconscious incompetent before you can startle the neighbors with your whiz-zoom speed and agility. That's why sales of helmets and knee guards are so high. We can't get to full competency, much less to step two in the printed instructions, until we master step one.

Challenges arise when we take up residence at Level #1 and don't move on. Whatever, your level of experience in sales, with this book you are an unconscious incompetent in terms of one-call closing. You won't master the strategies until you've finished reading the book—at least twice—and implemented the strategies in actual presentations with clients.

Let's compare this to something as simple and reflexive as driving. Assuming you do have a driver's license, you probably don't drive today as you did when you first had your learner's permit. You are most likely at Level #4 when it comes to driving. It's become an unconscious move to turn on your blinkers while navigating through your daily routes, right? If so, you would say you're an unconsciously competent driver.

Okay, let's say you're given a new driving experience. You are now sitting in the driver's seat at a NASCAR race. Do you know how to drive? Yes. Do you know how to drive a stock car at 200 miles an hour around a circular track without hitting something or causing bodily harm to yourself in some way? Probably not. In that context, are you at Level #4? No. You've just stepped back to Level #1.

The same applies to the strategies in this book.

Yesterday you may have been a master at the outdated techniques of high-pressure sales and today you are facing an entirely new way of doing business. Again, that's okay because you will move on to the next steps. Won't you?

Level #2, the *conscious incompetent*, is really a state of awareness. You vaguely know that there's a something better or different out there. You also are aware that you really don't know very much about it. At this level, you don't know everything you need to know about a subject. In other words, the conscious incompetent knows he or she doesn't know.

The people who are comfortable with Level #2 don't give it much thought. In fact, they avoid thinking about those nagging questions altogether. People who want to move on and up with life, people like you, will become quite curious at this level. You want to learn more, be more, do more, and have more.

If you're intimidated by the amount of information you must grasp, don't be. You will get where you are going. You will become a master of the one-time close because you have the drive and the discipline to achieve it.

And now you know that it's out there to be achieved. The fact that you are reading this book means that you are already at Level #2! Shoot, you're halfway there already.

Level #3, the *conscious competent*, is busy reading, studying, watching the experts, picking up new information, and learning everything he or she can about the subject at hand. The person at Level #3 is even experimenting, trying new things, and learning what works and what doesn't work quite so well. It's an exciting level because things are happening. Progress is being made. And you don't find yourself paralyzed by fear so often. In fact, long stretches of time pass without you even thinking about some of the many things that filled you with apprehension in the recent past.

Level #4, the *unconscious competent*, is the level of the master closer, the closing specialist. If you stick with this program, you will get there and probably a lot faster than you now believe. This is the ultimate experience. You are so knowledgeable and experienced that one-time closing is a natural process.

You barely have to think about it before you flawlessly execute your presentations. Your sales reflexes are so finely-honed that the process has become internalized. Your sales presentation is fine-tuned and targeted precisely to serving the unique needs of your clients with the unique solutions provided by your product or service.

Certainly, those nagging fears still drop in now and again, but they're way in the background. You know how to handle them. More than that, you *are* handling them.

Level #4 is a very heady place to be. You'll like it. Are you ready to grow to Level #4? Are you ready to become a one-time closing specialist? Only you know the answer. But we suspect it's a resounding *"Yes!"* And as an old radio announcer used to say, *"Ah, there's good news tonight."* You can achieve Level #4. You can master the art of the one-time close. All you have to do is follow three basic steps.

Step One—Become a Sales Champion

The word *"champion"* is so important that it became a key element in Tom's first company and it has always been an important aspect of his training philosophy. A champion is a person who is the best they can be at what they choose to do. Champions always strive to be better today than they were yesterday.

C Commitment

Commitment breeds competence. Comedian/filmmaker Woody Allen said that half the secret to success is just showing up. Showing up is one of the major commitments a champion makes. Without it, none of the other stages of success can possibly follow.

H *Honesty*

Be honest with all your words and actions. Having an honest work ethic is a requirement for success in business and in life. You can't be honest with your friends at church or at the civic club and then turn it off when you go to work. Either you are honest or you are not.

A *Attitude*

You get to choose your attitude about everything. So why not choose positivity? As with baseball great Babe Ruth, the person who hits the most home runs is also the person who likely holds the record for most strike-outs. That's just part of the job and a champion must be equipped to handle both failure and success. A positive attitude isn't just nice to have—it's essential equipment.

M *Mastery*

You can't sell what you don't know. But a champion knows more than just facts, and figures. He or she knows the product, the company, the industry, and the competition. They also develop the skills necessary to understand who the ideal clients are for the product. Then, they develop the skills and techniques of master salespeople

P *Persistence*

The word quit is just not in the vocabulary of a champion. It's not even in their dictionary or thesaurus! They live by Tom's words, *"You have not failed until you have stopped trying."*

I *Imagination*

Imagination is required to envision future success and the lifestyle it will provide. Right now the future resides within your imagination. What you "see" as the outcome of your efforts, success or failure, will determine that outcome. Every great advance of civilization throughout the history of the world was first developed in someone's imagination.

O   *Organization*

In a very real sense we cannot waste time—we can only waste ourselves. Time is fertile ground. We can let it lie fallow or we can plow, plant, harvest and feed the world.

N   *Non-judgmental*

Champions are far too focused on developing themselves as well-rounded, thoroughly professional human beings to waste time judging others. They just don't have time for it. (See the item directly above.)

Step Two—Turn Pro

Wherever you go, you will find champions of all stripes. Some champions are talented amateurs and others are true professionals. What's the difference? In a word, *"results."* The *professional* champion earns top dollar in his or her field. More than that, the professional has a profound sense of self-worth and usually the admiration of his or her peers.

Here are a few key tips on becoming a pro.

- *Develop a professional's attitude.* Your work is your profession deserving your respect and very best efforts. It's not "just a job."

- *Look like a professional.* From the tip of your highly-polished shoes to the top of your well-groomed head, you always look your best. Whether you are in farm and field or company jet and corporate HQ, people instantly know you're a pro just by your look.

- *Your business looks professional.* Your business cards are professionally designed and printed. You have a web presence that is visually appealing and full of valuable information. If you're on social media, you update your information on a regular basis (and way more frequently than once a month).

- *Organize like a professional.* Your presentation materials are well-organized, up-to-date and readily available. Fumbling for a chart, a document or some other material not only detracts from your presentation, it creates the impression that you are sloppy in your attention to detail.

- *Use the language professionals use.* Your verbal and written communication should always be appropriate to the situation and the client, but the use of foul language, slang, poor grammar or technical jargon is just unforgivable. Plain English is a universal and quite eloquent language.

- *Follow your profession.* It's important to know what's going on within your company, but it is equally important to know what's happening within your industry. Keep up or follow in the wake of those who do.

- *Keep on keeping on.* In other words, as a salesperson it is your job and your duty to sell—every day and at every appropriate opportunity. One of the most significant differences between a champion and an also-ran, is the champion's ability to make a call, knock on a door, approach a prospect, answer an inquiry, confirm appointments and make presentations while the others sit around the break room and gripe about the economy.

- *Adopt a professional's standards.* A professional is honest—period. The highest ethical standards of conduct and behavior are an essential aspect of the professional's very being. These rigorous standards apply

24-hours a day, seven days a week. There are no exceptions.

- *Have fun.* Selling is a demanding profession with great rewards, but it is something you should enjoy, really enjoy. A lot of people are delighted to go to the job every day because the job of selling is more challenging than most jobs. And, you get to meet and build relationships with interesting people all the time.

Step Three—Follow the Four P's

Those famous *"Breakfast of Champions"* commercials in which the pro athlete states, *"You better eat your Wheaties,"* can be viewed on two levels. The obvious one is that it's a wise and healthy idea to eat a good breakfast. The other level is more subtle and at the same time more dramatic. It pertains to an entire set of things the champion must accomplish in advance of claiming his or her position in the winner's circle. We call these the Four P's. The Four P's aren't a singing group from the sixties. They're guidelines to becoming a master of sales, especially of one-time closing.

Prepare—Practice—Perform—Perfect

Prepare. The one-time closing specialist is ready to meet the expected and the inevitable, unexpected challenges inherent in this business. The need to prepare was dramatically, and tragically illustrated in the book *"YEAGER"* by General Chuck Yeager and Leo Janos (Bantam Books).

If you haven't read or seen the movie, *"The Right Stuff,"* Chuck Yeager was a World War Two flying ace, the first man to break the sound barrier, and a true legend in aviation in his time. Yeager said that the skills and abilities that make a good fighter pilot did not automatically transfer to another field, such as test flying new, unproven, and very dangerous jets.

Nerves of steel, fast reflexes, and brilliant flying skills need to be balanced with other factors—preparation for each flight, for example. He notes the unnecessary loss of another great ace and test pilot, Richard Bong, who flamed out just 50 feet off the ground, too low for a successful parachute escape. Bong hadn't studied his pilot's manual and a simple mistake cost him his life. *"Dick wasn't interested in homework,"* said Yeager. Lack of preparation in sales may not cost you a life, but it could cost you a sale, a job, or even your career.

The one-time closer takes his or her homework very seriously.

Practice. Knowing what to do and doing it are entirely different things. Certainly, you would practice your piano prior to performing a concerto in public, wouldn't you? You'd practice for a weekend game of softball, an archery contest, or for a presentation to your civic club, right? Then you understand the need to practice your sales presentations.

Enlist the aid of a friend, loved one, or sales associate. Use a mirror and give a presentation to yourself. Use a video or audio recorder. Become thoroughly familiar with your presentation. Make it so much a part of you that it just flows naturally.

The old adage *"practice makes perfect"* is almost right. What if your practice isn't up to par? Suppose you practice poorly? We'd like to amend the adage to say, only *perfect practice* makes perfect. And if you don't achieve perfection, at the very least you'll be a lot more prepared than if you jumped into a presentation with *"Hi, I'm Bob. I know just what you need. Here's the product you've been waiting for. Sign this and it's yours."*

Ask Bob. He's now working part time making sandwiches down at the *House of Spam*.

Perform. Sooner or later, you have to get in there and mix it up with potential clients. Don't wait until you think you know enough or are good enough or you will prepare yourself right out of a job.

Regardless of our level of expertise or performance, we all have room for improvement. There's always something more to learn. Create your presentations to the best of your ability and get in front of clients. The best feedback you can get on your effectiveness is from living, breathing, qualified clients. Give it everything you've got. You'll win some and you'll lose some, but you will continue to improve because you will ...

Perfect. A one-time closing master never stops learning, especially from his or her own experiences. Make mental notes on every presentation. Evaluate each performance and invest the time to consider how to improve your weak areas. Make a serious study of yourself and your presentation. Then practice the Four Ps all over again: Prepare, Practice, Perform and keep on Perfecting!

One of the things we truly love about sales is that it is a field open to all. Whether you are male or female, young or old, a beanpole or pleasantly plump, regardless of your race, education, culture, or prior level of experience, you can be a champion in sales.

Real success in sales doesn't require any special God-given talent. You already have the ability. You don't need Tinkerbelle's magic dust, a spell from Merlin the Magician, or anyone's permisson. All you need is drive, commitment, discipline, and heart. We think that last item is most important. You can't measure the heart of a champion. It's just too big. They live to serve the needs of others through the vehicle of sales. Once you develop the heart of a champion, all the other items in the list will inevitably follow.

Sales Skills are Transferable

We have often heard a version of this statement, *"Why should I work so hard? I'm not going to stay in sales forever."* We offer two answers. One, anything, anything at all that you do you should do to the best of your ability. Two, the skills you learn in sales will serve you in every area of your life.

If you're going into politics, you will need to close the voters.

If you enter corporate America, you'll need to make presentations to your boss(es), clients, or customers. (Or, are you planning the rest of your career without ever asking for a promotion?)

Even if you're just planning retirement, you'll need sales skills to close your spouse on that summer-long tour of America's bass fishing havens or the *Yard-Sale-Across-America Experience.*

Sales skills are transferable. You can take them anywhere you go and put them to work building a better life. If nothing else, you'll improve the results you get when selling yourself to others as a friend, a volunteer, or an employee.

Let's Face Facts

And freeze-out fear. Once you have begun the continuing process of preparing, practicing, performing, and perfecting, you will begin to forget about your fears. Like those trouble-making cousins at the family picnic, fear will always be hanging around. But once you have mastered the Four Ps, you can pretty much ignore them. They just aren't much of a factor in your life anymore.

Forget your fear of loss. Loss will happen and it will happen to everyone except those timid souls who lack the courage to ever reach for the brass ring. Loss is a natural by-product of the sales process and a necessary step on the road to gain. So, when you occasionally lose, accept it, learn from it, let it go and move on.

Forget your fear of the past and move on into a bright, shining, and successful future. You no longer need to be held back by feelings of guilt, regret, or loss over whatever might have been. You can leave whatever happened before where it belongs—in the past. Just because it happened once doesn't mean you are doomed to repeat the experience. When you learn from your past negative experiences, you will to avoid those same pitfalls in the future. Even better, you know how to turn them into positive outcomes the next time.

Forget your fear of the unknown. We all face a certain amount of fear of the unknown. Once you master the art of the one-time sale, knowledge will defeat fear. Your experience and skill will allow you to put yourself in your buyer's shoes in order to discover the best way to serve his or her unique needs. The unknown will always be with us, but you will be able to control the situation because you'll be focused on the known system for lowering sales resistance and increasing sales acceptance.

Forget your fear of failure. Failure is nothing more than just another part of the game.

A newspaper editor once fired Walt Disney for a *"lack of ideas."*

Thomas Edison's teachers thought he was too stupid to learn.

As we noted earlier, Babe Ruth, with one of the best base-ball home run records, also holds the record for the most strike-outs. Those very public failures didn't keep him from becoming The Home Run King, did it?

The one-time closing specialist accepts failure when it occurs, evaluates what happened, learns from the experience, and moves on as a better salesperson for it. In other words, he or she tries again ... and again ... and again!

Tom says: You have not failed until you stop trying.

Forget your fear of the future. That's where we're all going to be living so why not do your very best to make that future as exciting, as productive and as satisfying as possible?

Forget your fear of making a mistake. You most certainly will make your share of mistakes. We all do. We all will. And, that's perfectly okay, provided we learn from them.

The fear of making a mistake can freeze a salesperson into inactivity. It can also push someone into a flurry of *misdirected* activity (a.k.a. busy work) just to avoid working with real-life buyers.

A champion doesn't fret over past mistakes or get stressed out over the possibility of future ones. He or she knows mistakes are excellent learning experiences and a natural part of the sales process. To paraphrase a famous quote, good salesmanship is built by way of experience, and experience is built by way of making mistakes. Go on. Get out there and earn your share. Start learning now!

And be sure to eat your Wheaties!

Tom says: If I could add an eleventh commandment, it would be "Thou shalt have no fear."

Pat says: Rarely, if ever, is our fear of a given calamity matched by the calamity itself. It is our fear that makes the thing worse than it ever needs to be.

CHAPTER 3

The Buyer's Mind

When preparing for the potential challenges of the one-time close, your chances of success multiply when you know and understand the mind of your buyer. Instinct is important, even essential, but it is not enough in and of itself. Remember the unfortunate experience of Dick Bong from the previous chapter. Instinct alone cannot replace knowledge. Because of that, the one-time closing specialist is serious about doing his or her homework.

Back in the 19th century, a brilliant man named Freud created an entire new field of medical science when he devoted his considerable energies to studying the various types of human personalities. The new science was dubbed psychology. Freud focused primarily on two types of people, the introvert and the extrovert.

Simply stated, an introvert is someone whose interest is primarily with his own thoughts and feelings. An extrovert is more concerned on the external physical or social environment. Neither one is inherently good or bad or better than the other. They are just two sides of the same human coin. One or the other will dominate your personality. Again, that's neither good nor bad; it's just what you make of it.

One-time closing requires insight, not necessarily expertise, into the personality of your potential client. The more you know, the better prepared you will be.

More important than that, you must develop a keen insight into your own personality. Whatever your own temperament, you must know how it will be received by other personalities. A champion is equally effective with the clients he likes and admires as he or she is with the folks with whom he feels different personality-wise. Remember, while we all want to make friends, our goal is first, and foremost to meet the needs of others.

Continued study of human personalities is essential for real, long-term success in sales. After all, that's a fundamental element of your work. You do sell your product to people, don't you?

Two personality types your studies will reveal are Type A or Type B. You probably have heard people remarking, *"Well, he's a Type A. What else would you expect?"* The Type A personality is more aggressive and assertive. This is the proverbial hard charger, most likely an extrovert.

Someone with a Type B personality is more laid back and introverted. *"Nothing ruffles her feathers"* or *"He just takes it as it comes"* might be said of this type. Again, neither is better or worse than the other—just different. And you must know how to recognize and work well with each.

The more you study, the more breakdowns and definitions of personality types you will encounter. For the purposes of this book, we will investigate the one-time closing process with four basic types of personalities.

The Four Basic Personality Types

The chart below shows the wide variations of personality types you will encounter. You will have to work with each type many times throughout your career. Salespeople aren't allowed to pick and choose the nature of their clients. That's why it's so important to recognize personalities and be adaptable. The time you invest in learning about them will pay off again and again.

You don't have to dig into a deep, theoretical text or sign up for a psychology course at the community college to understand the various types of human personalities. Just think of the differences in terms of people you already know.

For example, if you are a driver, you will have a tendency to mold your sales presentations into a format that fits your profile. This may work well with the other drivers you approach. What about the rest?

By understanding the different types of personalities, including your own, you can adapt your style to meet the unique needs of each situation. This is not to say that you *become* another person. You can't. Just realize that the needs of your potential clients come first, far ahead of your need to appear to be running the show, and act accordingly.

Conversely, an amiable personality might have to become a bit more assertive when working with another amiable. Two people of this type may end up being great friends, but the occurrence of a sale is unlikely. Forewarned is forearmed. Whatever the personality mix at the time, your knowledge of personality types will allow you to step out of your own skin, to better meet the needs of your buyers.

Regardless of your own personal style or the style of your buyers and clients, with proper knowledge you can adapt to fit any situation. Again, you don't become a separate and false person to manipulate an unsuspecting buyer. You just change your delivery to meet the personality of each individual so you can best serve his or her needs.

Why You Shouldn't Go Fishing
with Strawberries

There's a wonderful example of the value of putting the needs of our buyers ahead of our own in Dale Carnegie's *"How to Win Friends and Influence People."* He writes about a salesman who didn't enjoy performing a particular part of the sales process. He preferred to jump ahead to what he considered more important areas.

At one point in his career, this salesman was asked if he ever went fishing. He said, *"yes"* and in fact, he loved the sport. He was then asked what bait he used. *"Night crawlers,"* he said.

Later in the conversation our fishing salesman mentioned that he was particularly fond of strawberries. At this point, he was asked if he ever used strawberries for fishing bait. *"Of course not!"* he said. *"Why not?"* was the immediate question. *"Because the fish don't like strawberries!"* And his own answer made the questioner's point. Just because you like something, doesn't mean the other party likes that same thing.

It is critical that we comprehend the likes and dislikes of the person to whom we are making a presentation so we can determine if our product or service is truly good for them before we attempt to close them.

Observe All Warning Signs

Smart automobile drivers pay attention to the speed limit and other warning signs on the highway because they know that it is not only obeying the law, but it is also the safest and overall the fastest way to their destination. Buyers post their own warning signs and it is just as important to obey the laws of sales.

Pay attention to the demeanor of your potential clients and adjust yours accordingly. It's a bit like acting on the stage. You play to the audience.

If you're making a presentation to a laid back audience, an overly-energetic performance with a lot of action and fast-paced speech could lose them. Conversely, if you have an upbeat, enthusiastic prospect, a mellow presentation could turn them off before you get to the high point of your presentation.

The ideal approach is to observe your prospect's demeanor. Mirror the speed and pitch in his or her voice. Subconsciously, this sends a message that, *"Hey, we're alike."* Additionally, your prospect will automatically understand you better.

If someone is a very slow speaker, adjust your rate so that it is just slightly faster. Do not, however, mimic someone's accent. Even if you're a terrific actor on the community stage, you'll never fool a potential client. He or she will be insulted and you'll be injured by your own poor judgment.

Also, while you will use different words, phrases and references with different audiences, never talk down to anyone.

Pat says: *Don't become so wrapped up in winning the battle of selling that you lose the war of selling* ***now.***"

Yes, it is important to know and understand the different personality types you will encounter. It's important to know and to plan out how your own temperament will interact with others. Yet, having said that, we don't want you to fall down the slippery slope of paying so much attention to personality only to leave yourself no time for the business of working toward the close. That's a very real and serious danger.

Completely changing your presentation based on each new client's personality would make the one-time close quite challenging, if not impossible. But you don't have to do that. Ideally, you've mastered a proven presentation, something that is effective for you and demonstrates your product effectively. The presentation might even be something carefully designed and fine-tuned by your company for very specific reasons. Changing it rapidly would disrupt the flow of your time with your clients and might even achieve the exact opposite of what the company had in mind.

Rather than structuring your presentation around the personality of the future client, you must be prepared to adjust your style and delivery to your customers' mindset. In other words, if they're open and interested, you'd match that mode. If they're hesitant and somewhat holding back or even fighting you a bit, you may have to give your presentation a bit more methodically in order to win them over.

This is where practicing your presentation over and over pays off. You don't want to use up so much time customizing or changing your presentation that you run out of time for one-time closing. Believe us. It happens.

The sales situation is moving along nicely; the conversation is flowing both ways; and the salesperson strikes the wrong chord. Somehow, despite all that planning, he or she manages to say the wrong thing.

Out of nowhere old Mr. Fear, and Mrs. Insecurity pop into the buyer's mind and stall the sale. They keep it from happening today. It may be unfortunate, but it is still a reality—we one-time closers don't have the luxury of unlimited time. Neither do we have the luxury of multiple visits that allow time to recover from a faux pas, regroup, and come back from another angle. Because of the ever-changing dynamics of sales and human personalities, the one-time closer must prepare strategies and potential adjustments to be able to quickly and smoothly match the buyer's mindset.

There are only two to choose from. Then, it just becomes a matter of changing gears, as necessary—smoothly and effortlessly. So you need to have a solid understanding of how things work ahead of time—enough of an understanding to be able to adapt on the fly.

That's not an impossible task. In fact, it's relatively straightforward when you follow the principles in this book.

Our system is successful for a very simple, yet powerful reason. When you place your potential clients into a sales situation, most will react in a certain manner that is universally consistent. Their individual personality types are important, but not a huge factor in the success or failure of your one-call closing presentation. And that fact doesn't contradict the preceding pages. You still need to know the different types and how to interact with them. We have just eliminated the necessity of investing too much time on that process.

In other words, this process lets you *sell it today, sell it now.*

💬 Level The Playing Field With The Level Of Your Presentation

As we've said, you never talk down to anyone. You *will* adapt your words, phrases, expressions, and references to each prospect.

A young kid with a GED deserves just as much attention and respect when he walks into your showroom as a Summa Cum Laude CEO. Without talking down (or up) to either, you will obviously adjust your presentation according to the needs of each. Know enough about your prospect going into your presentation so that you can talk on his or her level.

What does that mean?

Let's look at two different couples walking in to buy a new refrigerator. Couple number one is a retired man and his wife who want to replace their 20-year old fridge.

What do you say to them?

The words *"fixed income"* probably come to mind. We'll assume you've asked a few qualifying questions to determine their specific needs which are likely to center around economy. Therefore, you'll want to discuss such topics as dependability, low energy costs, longer food storage capabilities which stretch the food budget and perhaps a service plan that can eliminate unexpected repair costs.

Couple number two is young and just starting out.

Would you use the same approach? No.

You would accentuate the features and benefits that apply to their specific situation. The features on the unit may be the same, but you will present the benefits in a different light, one viewed from their perspective.

For example, they may be cost conscious, like the older couple, and want to look at lower-priced models. You even may refer them to the same model the other couple chose, but you would handle it differently as they may be more interested in features such as outside water and ice dispensers. You may even win them over to a larger model with a higher investment when they realize the longevity of the higher quality brands. The slightly greater investment they make now will likely be offset by the replacement cost they'll avoid down the road. In truth, the larger unit may be the most cost-effective decision.

In other words, a one-time closer speaks a lot of different languages. You speak old folks. You speak young family. You speak CEO and you speak GED.

The language all depends upon the needs of the individual buyer. If you want to test this, try talking in normal business terms to a five year old. He or she will lose interest almost immediately. But then try speaking on the child's level and just watch the happy animation appear on that tiny face as he or she realizes you have just entered the five-year old world. It's like magic. And the same technique will work magic in sales

The Buyer Mindset

When put into a sales scenario, the buyer's mindset subconsciously asks important questions which must be answered before they are comfortable moving ahead with the sales process. Because this is a *sub*conscious process, we know that it is always at work. We can count on it. More than that, we can make it our ally.

How often have you heard yourself, or others saying the words, *"I'm just looking"* when approached by a salesperson? It doesn't matter what the buyer's individual personality style may be, this is a universal, knee-jerk reaction because of the mindset change we all undergo when a sales scenario starts.

We are thinking, *"I don't need you, your product or service;" "I don't have any reason to trust what you have to say;" "I don't need any help to determine if you have a product or service that interests me;"* and *"I'm in no hurry to make a decision."* So, basically, *"Let me shop by myself, thank you."*

The insights we will cover on those four thoughts, which, we remind you, are consistent in every selling situation, will help you quickly lower sales resistance and increase sales acceptance. Thus reaching the goal of a closed sale today.

The following four words, and the questions they bring to your customer's mind, control every sales situation: Need, Trust, Help, Hurry.

Here's how.

NEED

"I feel no need." Your goal as a one-call closer is to help them change their mindset to one of *"I feel some need."*

TRUST

"*I feel no trust.*" No one will let you persuade them to do or own anything if they don't trust you. So, you must work toward helping them think, "*I feel some trust.*"

HELP

"*I want no help.*" No one ever wants to admit they're helpless. However, you can certainly help someone see that you can provide answers in areas where they may not be as educated as you are. After all, you are a trained professional in your field. So, you need to change their mindset to one of "*I want some help.*"

HURRY

"*I feel no hurry.*" Your job is to help them see that by taking care of the buying decision today, they'll be better off than if they wait. They need to think, "*I feel some hurry*" in order to take action.

All Sales are Controlled by Need-Trust-Help-Hurry

That's it. When you master the concept of Need-Trust-Help-Hurry you are well on your way to mastering the art of one-time closing. It is extremely important that you learn how these four very specific words help define your potential client's sales resistance. They are the primary barrier between *"no sale"* and *"sale."* They are the main line of defense. They will keep you from providing the prospective client the very product or service they agreed to talk over with you and/or need the most. These four words are powerful enough to keep your future client from making a purchase right now. And right now is the timeframe that concerns us most.

Viewed from the perspective of a professionally trained salesperson, it is your duty to overcome the walls put up by those four words. Mastery over Need-Trust-Help-Hurry will allow you to alter the prospect's mindset, thus helping him or her make a decision that's truly good for them—today. By mastering this concept, not only will you be a conscious competent, but you'll have a head start on becoming an unconscious competent—a master closer.

The Four Horsemen of the Apocalypse Now

Think about this. You only have four obstacles between *"no sale"* and *"Where do I sign?"* All the sales resistance in the world can be boiled down to those four simple words. No matter whom you approach, the size of the company, the title of the person on the door, you only face a maximum of four obstacles. That should bring you an incredible sense of relief. And power.

It's similar to the situation a football coach faces. No matter how big the organization behind the team may be, there are never more than eleven players on the field, no more, no less. That simple fact alone eliminates a lot of unnecessary stress. The disadvantage is that he or she never knows exactly where those players will be after *"one-two-three hike!"* Of course, the opposing coach has the same challenge, so things have a way of balancing out.

Mastering the art of the one-time close gives you the edge because you will already know all the defense's options. We have given you a look at the opposing team's playbook and all you have to do is run your own well-planned game.

Speaking of running, let's look at your enviable position from the point of view of track and field. There you are in your running togs and your feather-light shoes. The gun sounds. Pow! You're off and running your heart out. One hundred yards later you spread your arms, smile, and pose for the winning photograph snapped by the local newspaper reporter.

But wait a minute. Something's terribly wrong here.

The other runners dash right past you and keep up their pace. Someone forgot to tell you what kind of race you're running. Clearly, it's not a 100-yard dash. Is it the 880-meter run, the mile, or the 26-mile marathon through Boston?

Makes a difference, doesn't it? Even the best runner would be severely handicapped not knowing the distance to be run before the race. How could you pace yourself? Evaluate the other runners' strategies? Know when to hold back and when to sprint for the finish line?

That's why it's so important to know what type of race you are to run before you take that first step off the blocks. The way the one-time closing specialist does that is to enter the mind of the prospect—by determining the potential client's personality type.

Is he or she an analytical, a driver, an amiable, or an expressive? Then, after planning and preparing your presentation for the prospect's mindset, you will plan and prepare your presentation by adapting your personality to meet the needs of the other party's personality.

If a driver is required, regardless of your own personality, you will become compatible with a driver. They will react with the Buyer Mindset and you will then proceed with the sales situation in accordance with the system outlined here— smoothly, flawlessly and almost effortlessly.

Now that you're off and running, there's even more good news. You don't have to worry about what kind of race you're running—in sales there are only these two: *buyer-initiated* and *salesperson-initiated*. We'll take a more in-depth look at them in the next chapter.

CHAPTER 4

The Two Formations of Personality Obstacles

The more we examine the four key defense measures of Need-Trust-Help-Hurry, the easier our race becomes to run. The four defenses can be arranged in only one of two formations. You are never in the position of the football coach or the runner who still must guess at the opposing strategy. You know you face the same strategies every time you go out. All you have to do is open your playbook, and adjust your presentation to the challenge at hand.

What Determines These Two Defense Formations?

That's an excellent question. We'll answer with another. Who initiated the sale?

There can be only one of two answers:

1. The buyer initiated the sale or

2. The salesperson initiated the sale.

As the cartoon character Porky Pig would say, *"That's all folks."* Knowing who initiated the sales process is one of the most important aspects of designing your presentation. And it's not hard to figure out, is it?

A buyer-initiated sale means the buyer has already taken some steps toward becoming a client. He or she has left the comfort of the easy chair, the distractions of the media, and the other concerns of the day. This potential future client may come to you as a walk-in to your showroom, an inquiry on your web page, an email, letter, or a phone call.

What form the inquiry takes isn't as important as the fact that your potential client believes it's time to consider buying something. At this stage of the game, he or she is already feeling some NEED.

There's already at least a bit of TRUST because he or she took the first step and it was toward you, right? Clearly, this person recognizes a need for some HELP and may even be in a HURRY to get it.

> *"My car broke down last night and I have to be on the road tomorrow. I NEED some help. My cousin said I could TRUST you folks to HELP me with a rental in a HURRY."*

A salesperson-initiated sale is quite different. Here the seller makes the first inquiry with a cold call. You may walk-in to their office, call on the phone, or approach someone who is *"just browsing, thanks."*

In these situations, the buyer is feeling NO TRUST, NO NEED, wants NO HELP, and is in NO HURRY. Do you get the impression that you will not exactly be greeted with open arms? But you knew you had your work cut out for you when you initiated the contact in the first place, so there's no surprise there anyway.

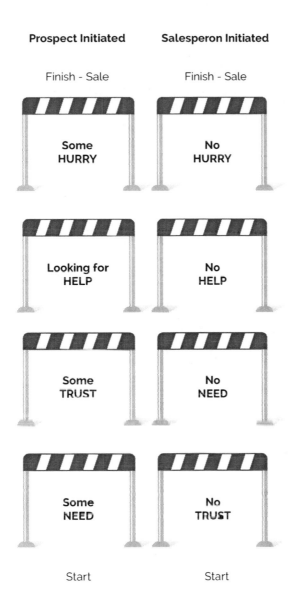

Prospect Initiated **Salesperon Initiated**

Finish - Sale   Finish - Sale

Some   No
HURRY   HURRY

Looking for   No
HELP   HELP

Some   No
TRUST   NEED

Some   No
NEED   TRUST

Start   Start

Notice that we have repositioned the words *need* and *trust* between the two examples. That's because your buyer has changed his or her mindset. This is important because the buyer's thought patterns have become more important than the personality you are approaching.

The prospect slides into a defensive mode the second you start your presentation, sometimes sooner. Often, you can see a physical change from across the showroom floor as you walk over or even catch it in their tone of voice as the person on the other end of the line realizes the reason for your call.

Don't worry. Remember, you are a master of one-call closing.

Jumping the High Hurdles

Some of the most exciting events in track and field are the high hurdles. Not only are the runners in a fast-paced race, they have to jump obstacles every so many yards. Getting to the one-call close is a lot like that.

So let's look at the mindset of your potential client in terms of a 100-yard high hurdle race.

Prospect Initiated

Finish - Sale

Some
HURRY

Looking for
HELP

**100 Yard
High Hurdles**

Some
TRUST

Some
NEED

Start

Hurdling the Buyer-Initiated Sale

The first hurdle is your buyer's *need* for your product or service. He (or she), obviously, feels some need or you wouldn't have received the e-mail inquiry, letter, phone call or walk-in visit. You will encounter various degrees of need.

"My Internet service just crashed. Again! I need to get back online today or I'll be out of business."

Obviously, you will handle the needs of this individual a bit differently from the person who drops by to browse and who has no immediate need to swap recipes online with Cousin Francie back east.

The second high hurdle is *trust*. Again, some trust has already been expressed. You know this simply because of the call or visit. The buyer has heard of your company through advertising, word-of-mouth or a very specific recommendation of a trusted friend and they've shown up at your door.

An important part of your job description is to start proving the value of that trust and to make it even stronger. Start building trust immediately. Do it with every question, every statement, and every gesture you make.

Examples:

"We carry the finest line of vacuum cleaners recommended by Consumers Digest magazine."

"We've been helping families like yours take charge of their financial futures for over 20 years."

"Our company takes great pride in its high customer satisfaction rate. Let me show you some of the comments our clients have made about our service."

"A reputation for professionalism is important when seeking out someone to help you sell your home, isn't it?"

Next, you have to jump the hurdle of *help*. The buyer is knocking on your door. So there's already some hope that you will be of help in resolving his or her challenge. Your task is to find out how, show how, and then prove the wisdom of your buyer's trust in you and your organization.

The last hurdle is *hurry*. There will be variables here. The buyer facing a major business loss has a significantly greater sense of urgency to get online than someone who is just beginning the research process for your type of product.

We want to encourage and enhance that sense of urgency. Even if it is just a tiny seed, we need to help it grow. The researcher may not be in any particular hurry, but you can change that. Show him the limited-time discounts, the end-of-the month special, the factory rebate, the dollars-off coupon or offer to "talk with the manager" for some special arrangement. You can easily, and legitimately, create a sense of urgency even when one does not initially exist.

Here are a few examples of how the buyer-initiated sale works.

1.   A Top Restaurant

Need — *"I feel hungry. Don't you?"*

Trust — *"Upscale's Restaurant has great food, don't you think?"*

Help — *"Their menu offers great food at reasonable prices. And it's not in French."*

Hurry — *"Let's beat the rest of the after-the-concert crowd."*

2.   A Grocery Store

Need — *"I'm throwing a big party."*

Trust — *"Kroger's is a good store."*

Help — *"Their deli has a variety of party food."*

Hurry — *"Party trays are 15% off with our coupon that expires this week."*

3.   A Clothing Store

Need — *"A new job demands a new suit."*

Trust — *"Macy's carries my favorite name brands."*

Help — *"The store features a big-and-tall section for folks like me."*

Hurry — *"The Fall sale ends today."*

4.   An Automobile Dealership.

Need — *"Well, it looks like "Old Bessie" has seen better days."*

Trust — *"Ajax Chevrolet has always treated me fairly."*

Help — *"Ajax has a really big selection, new and used."*

Hurry — *"It's the end of the month. I bet I can get a great price."*

The Salesperson-Initiated Sale

We're still running. We're still jumping, but the situation has changed quite a bit. As we noted, the sales process begins with a series of emotions, pre-conceived ideas and thoughts. Some are valid and some are way off the mark. Those emotions, especially the ones off the mark, become defenses. Fortunately for our coach/runner/salesperson, those hurdles are arranged in a particular order. As a master of the one-time close, you aren't going to allow yourself to become tripped up as you race toward the finish line.

The order of hurdles (defenses) for the salesperson-initiated sale is different from the buyer-initiated sale.

Salesperon Initiated

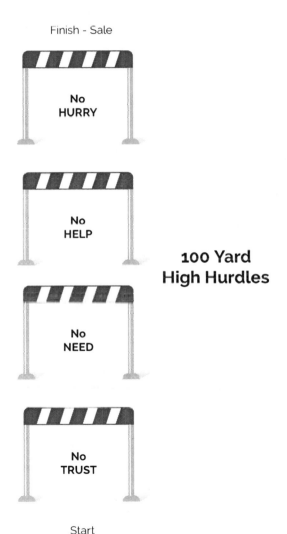

Finish - Sale

No
HURRY

No
HELP

**100 Yard
High Hurdles**

No
NEED

No
TRUST

Start

In the salesperson-initiated sale, there's no trust at all. The buyer doesn't know enough to trust, and the salesperson even lacks a foundation for building trust. Lack of trust is the first emotion buyers feel.

She (or he) doesn't know you, your company (at least very well), your product or service, whether you provide good service after the sale, etc. In other words, your starting place is called ground zero.

The good news is that being so low; the only way to go is up, right? Yes—provided you follow the principles of the one-time close. Otherwise, you're stuck at ground zero indefinitely.

To build trust, your presentation must include pertinent information on:

- You

- Your company

- What you've done that makes you knowledgeable about the subject

- What you will do for your individual customer.

In other words, what's the buyer's payoff for investing their valuable time with you?

Once you're past that hurdle, you face the prospect's lack of need.

"I don't really know that much about your product. I don't see how it will do anything for me at the moment. I've lived this long without it. I have other, more important needs at this time."

Don't worry. Because you are a master of one-time closing and you know that you don't really face hurdles. These so-called defenses are really opportunities for you to gain more insight into the needs of your buyer. Used properly and put in their proper perspective, they help you keep the dialog going. Think of them as guideposts to the close.

Then, of course, your buyer can't actually see how you, your product or your company can be of that much help, if at all. Your buyer may listen attentively, nod in the affirmative, scan your brochures, and still not believe you have the right solution for the situation at hand. She doesn't believe you can help her.

This is where having testimonials from satisfied clients comes in handy. Show her proof of how you have helped someone else in similar circumstances, and she just might change her mind about what you can do for her.

The final hurdle is the fact that she isn't in a hurry. There's no real sense of urgency to make the purchase. *"The last thing I'd ever dream of is making a purchase right now."* Of course, your task is to prove to her the significant value of making a purchase right now. That's how her dream, whatever it may be, can come true with your expert help.

Here is an example of how someone who doesn't use one-time closing mis-handles a salesperson-initiated sale by telephone. Let's call her "Jane."

RINGGGGGG.

CONSUMER: *"Hello."*

Jane: *"Hello, my name is Jane and I'm calling from Acme Deluxe Heating and Air Conditioning."*

CONSUMER: *"What was your company's name again?"*

No Trust

Jane: *"We're offering a special on duct cleaning to homeowners in your area who will allow us to show our new Mega-Pro Widgett that can cut your fuel bills in half."*

CONSUMER: *"Thanks, but we really don't need a, what did you call it, a Widgett, right now."*

No Need

Jane: *"Oh, I see—you must be happy with your current fuel bill, then. Well, for the time we've shared together, we will still offer you the free duct cleaning. We could have someone out there Wednesday. Would morning or evening be better for you?"*

CONSUMER: *"I really don't think we need any service right now."*

No Help

Jane: *"This really is a unique opportunity."*

CONSUMER: *"Well, why don't you call back next spring, okay?"*

No Hurry

Jane was polite, professional, informative, enthusiastic and what else?

Jane was unsuccessful. She didn't make a sale, an appointment or even much of an impression because she wasn't using knowledge of the prospect's mindset to get over all those hurdles the consumer placed between her and the finish line.

Let's see how June, the one-call closing specialist, would handle the same situation.

RINGGGGGG.

CONSUMER: *"Hello."*

SALESPERSON: *"Hello, My name is June and I'm calling from Acme Deluxe Heating and Air Conditioning, the area's leader for more than a quarter of a century."*

CONSUMER: *"Oh, I think I've heard of you."*

Some Trust

SALESPERSON: *"You're aware of the rising cost of fuel these days, aren't you?"*

CONSUMER: *"Who isn't?"*

Some Need

SALESPERSON: *"That's why I'm calling. We're offering a free demonstration of our Mega-Pro Widgett that can cut fuel bills in half."*

CONSUMER: *"In half? You can really do that?"*

Some Help

SALESPERSON: *"Yes, ma'am, and we have hundreds of letters from satisfied customers to document that."*

CONSUMER: *"Fifty percent is quite a saving."*

SALESPERSON: *"We're offering a special, one-time rate on duct cleaning as part of this special offer. Would Wednesday morning or evening be best for you?"*

CONSUMER: *"Morning is best. Tell me more about that special."*

Some Hurry

The process really is that simple when you follow the proper procedure. Regardless of who initiates the sale, you now have a full understanding of the dynamics involved. Knowing the consumer's mindset and the sequence of feelings that will set up his or her defenses, allows you to jump every hurdle, reach the finish line, and close the sale.

Now that you know about the hurdles before you, let's start developing the skills in greater depth that you'll need in order to jump them. We'll start with building trust in Chapter Five.

CHAPTER 5

Trust everybody, but cut the cards
~ **Finley Peter Dunne,** *Mr. Dooley's Philosophy*

The First Defense—Trust
Part I

An old, back country fisherman decides he needs a new lure or two for the old tackle box. He heads into town for a tour of the sporting goods section of the fancy new department store. He invests fifteen or twenty minutes looking over the turquoise trappers, the greeney-goo grabbers, and the star spangled lip lockers, finally deciding on a particularly evil-looking collection of hooks and spangles.

"Do the fish really like this contrivance," he asks.

"I don't know," says the salesperson. *"I don't sell to fish."*

That's a good point, but one that's not likely to encourage a sale. The only way that salesperson will ever sell a "ruby red raptor" or anything else to the experienced, old fisherman is to use one of his most precious assets—trust.

But before he (or she) can use it, he has to earn it.

Measuring the Initial Level of Trust

Realistically, you can't measure the level of trust a buyer feels with any degree of accuracy until you get feedback. That feedback can be in the form of direct answers, by the way the buyer dodges questions, or even through body language. A one-call closing master is always monitoring the buyer or client for those vital signs.

But what about those precious seconds before you can get any real feedback?

Actually, you can see some pretty good indicators even before the first *"Hello."* For example, a buyer who holds back, looks nervously around, or won't look you in the eye is probably severely lacking in the trust department.

Then again, the buyer may have a lot of trust, but may also be terribly shy or just intimidated by a lack of knowledge about your product or your company. Handling the situation according to the one-time closing process will soon provide you with the answers you seek. But regardless of the individual or the circumstances, one of two levels of trust will always be present:

1. Some trust

2. No trust at all

It is important that you discover which is which immediately. Is the glass half full? Or is it dry as a bone and dusty from lack of use? Is it cracked and chipped from earlier experience and in need of repair? Is it merely half full, waiting for you to top it off with your professionalism and skill?

What Do We Know and When Do We Know It?

When the buyer initiates the sale, you can safely assume there is at least some level of trust present. After all, he or she would never have picked up the phone, clicked into your website, or walked in the door otherwise.

The level of trust could be significant. That's especially true when the buyer has been referred by a trusted friend. *"Uncle George said I could trust you to outfit Uncle Bob's new tackle box for me. What do you recommend for somebody who fishes for catfish?"*

On the other hand, the level of trust could be at best, shall we say, anemic. *"I don't know you...I don't know your product...I don't know your company... I don't know your capabilities...I don't know your reputation...I don't even know your industry... NOW SELL ME."*

That's okay. You can work with the situation, any situation, once you define it. Even if the level of trust borders on the miniscule, the one-call closing master will do everything possible to: (1) maintain that level of trust from the first instance of contact, and (2) start filling up that glass of trust until it is overflowing. You will do everything in your power to build on whatever foundation you are provided. And you will start building right away.

How Much Trust is Enough?

The quick answer is all you can get. More important for the salesperson, initially, is to realize that you don't have to earn all the trust in the world in the first ten seconds of your approach. That's totally unnecessary and, worse, making that kind of intensive effort will probably backfire on you. Your buyer could start thinking, *"If this salesperson is so concerned about trust there must be some problem here. Hey, I don't trust this guy!"*

Initially, the salesperson should achieve enough trust so the buyer will listen to the rest of the presentation and believe the salesperson is not only truthful, but has the client's best interests at heart. At first, that's all you have to do. Establish that basic level and build from there.

When you continue your presentation according to one-call closing principles, the trust will inevitably grow. Your buyer will soon have no qualms about purchasing the product because you will determine his or her unique need and will demonstrate why your product is the best solution.

Gaining trust requires five sequential steps. Note: each step must be taken *in its proper order.* To do otherwise is like preparing an omelet by putting the eggs in before the cooking oil. Oh, things will heat up all right, but you'll most certainly have a rather sticky and unpleasant experience in your pan.

To be so hard to come by, trust is remarkably easy to lose. Here's a perfect example from the not too distant past. Back in the days before plastic was so common, many of the components of everyday life were made of rubber, including toys. Parents really appreciated that because kids had a hard time destroying toys made from such a durable product.

A nationally-known media personality who had a reputation for integrity (and who shall remain nameless) advertised a very low price for soft rubber toys ideal for young children. Many parents, surprised and delighted by such a low price on such a sturdy item, ordered the soft rubber toys.

In case you didn't see this coming, the toys turned out to be colored balloons in animal shapes that were stuck through a square piece of cardboard which provided a base. In most homes, those toys lasted less than a day. Now, it is true the media personality did not technically lie, but he still broke the bond of trust between himself and his audience. Many of those parents never purchased another item advertised by that personality again.

Once lost, trust proves amazingly difficult to regain. The one-call closing specialist gains that trust and holds onto it dearly, like the precious treasure it is.

Let's Play *"Who Don't You Trust?"*

You want to create a situation where you can safely and realistically think *"my buyers like me. They trust me, and they want to listen to me."* Obviously, *no trust* is much more difficult to handle than *some trust*. It's a much more extreme condition and *extreme* is no exaggeration. That's why we're addressing that little scenario first.

We'll show you how to master each of the five trust-building steps to the fullest. Each step reduces sales resistance by 10 degrees. Soon, you'll be establishing a bond of trust with even the most difficult, least trusting buyer or client. At that point, you'll not only be a master at working with no-trust personalities. Working with the some-trust person will be a breeze.

We'll elaborate now on our five trust-building steps, tossing in a few real-world role-plays to make our points. Please, if you're in a business in which the potential client always initiates the sale, don't skip over this section. If you're like the rest of us inhabitants of the sales universe, there's always a lot more to learn. You'll pick up valuable information by learning these important no-trust steps and will be in a much better position to serve your some-trust buyers and clients.

The Five Steps to Gaining Trust

The five steps to gaining trust are:

1. Propriety

2. Intent Statement

3. Commonality

4. Credibility

5. Competency

Step #1 - Propriety Your Appearance and Actions Must Always Fit the Situation

The word propriety comes from two root words:

● Proper

● Appropriate

Propriety, according to one of the definitions in Webster's Unabridged Dictionary, means *"conformity with what is proper or fitting."* In other words, for something to possess propriety, it must fit the situation. Your organization, you and your fellow salespeople, and your support materials must all fit your job responsibilities and the image your company wants portrayed in the world. Everything must be proper and appropriate. Otherwise, things tend to fall apart in a most embarrassing and costly way.

The clothing you wear as part of your job is a perfect example. As a general rule, we believe in dressing the part. Suit, tie, well-pressed pants or skirt, and shoes polished to an eye-stinging, near-painful glare are usually essential elements of the dress code for sales. But a general rule doesn't always apply to specific situations.

For example, what's wrong with the following mental picture? The owner of a small farm tractor dealership starts out his day in a sharp three-piece suit, new tie, polished shoes, etc. The first thing on his to-do list is a visit to his bank's loan department for a business expansion loan. Is he dressed properly—appropriate to the situation? Your answer is—yes, he is. There is absolutely nothing at all wrong with this picture. And you are absolutely correct.

Now let's change the scene—same owner, same outfit. This time he's visiting the largest farmer in the valley in the hope of selling a brand new $75,000 Dirt-Slinger 2000. Naturally, the farmer is a working man, working on his farm, which is to say working way down there in the dirt. Here comes our well-dressed dealer slopping through the furrows and losing his formerly-polished, now ruined shoes in the mud to shake hands with his potential client.

What kind of impression is he making? Is his dress appropriate to the situation? Of course not. The farmer likely takes our overdressed owner for *"a dang fool"* for coming out in a muddy field dressed like that. The salesperson has just lost credibility due to his attire being inappropriate.

In this situation, the perfect dress for one part of his job is totally out of place in another. Being overdressed could cost him the sale because the farmer won't trust the opinion of someone who is not like him—much less someone showing a remarkable lack of common sense.

Normally, you wouldn't expect a successful business owner to be wearing blue jeans and scruffy work boots to make a big sale, but if that sale takes place out in the north forty, that dress is entirely appropriate.

Conversely, if our tractor dealer's appointment with the banking committee is in the afternoon, he'd be well advised to clean up his act and get back into the suit before making his presentation. Bankers may appreciate the value of the north forty, but they don't want any of it on their expensive carpet.

Your total personal profile including clothing, hairstyle, jewelry, body language, and conversational style should be in sync with your buyer's perception of what you should be. You don't want to mimic what they're wearing, but you don't want to be dressed in an extremely different manner either.

Example #1: Ringing Up a No-Sale

You are enjoying your favorite television program when you hear your doorbell ring. You peer out the tiny door viewer. Someone is staring back, his face curved by the magnifying glass. Even with that distorted view, you know this is a stranger. You open the door cautiously. The man is dressed very casually. His clothing is not very clean and is in need of a good pressing. You stop counting body piercings at number fifteen and are glad your door doesn't have a built-in metal detector. The man's awkward stance with his weight on one hip cries out *"hurry up, man, I got places to go!"* You do not want to talk to this man. You don't want to hear anything he has to say and you don't want to look at him any longer than you absolutely have to—which isn't very long at all because you say *"we already gave"* and shut the door in his unshaven face.

It is safe to say the man's total lack of propriety turned you off. There was never even a chance for him to begin a presentation, much less to start building trust.

Example #2: A Ringing Endorsement

As you're settling back into your favorite chair, the bell rings again. This time when you peer through the viewer things appear much more positive. You see a well-dressed young woman. She stands courteously back from the door so you can see who's come to call. She is looking away so you can get a good profile of who's knocking at your door. She is wearing a warm smile, and is professionally and neatly dressed. Instead of *"We already have given..."* you're thinking *"I wonder what brought her to my door tonight? Who is this person and what is she selling?"*

In other words, the person who is proper and appropriate just made a good first impression. There is at least a foundation for building trust.

How many times have you been approached by a salesperson who asked if you needed any help? Often, of course, but how many times have you said, *"No, thanks, I'm just looking"* just to get rid of the person because the first impression they gave was so negative you didn't want to encourage him or her? Now, ask yourself if you have ever made such a bad impression. Hmm. Maybe that's why we wonder why some of our buyers are not more receptive to our ideas.

Before we go to work (in the showroom, knocking on doors, driving a route, etc.) we should always pause to ask, *"Dressed like this, will I get any doors slammed in my face?"* If your answer is *"yes,"* then you need a dose of propriety before going one step further.

Act the Part to Get the Part

It's sad, but true, from the moment you make contact with a potential or existing client, you are being judged visually, verbally, and even intuitively. Remember, anything that *can* be judged will be judged. Fair or not, that's just a fact of doing business and that's why acting the part to get the part is so critical.

We remember a terrific television and film character actor of the past who played every type of character including Mexicans, Spaniards, Native Americans, Italians, Anglos, peasants, banditos, business tycoons, and lots of your average Joes. In other words, he played just about any part a man could play. In an article published about him, he shared one of the secrets of his success.

Whenever reading for a part, he always dressed and got into makeup *for the part*. Of course, he didn't get every role he ever read for, but he got more than his competitors. Why? Because of all the actors trying out for any given part his dress and make up (and talent, of course) made him appear to be the ideal person to fit the role.

During casting calls, his *selling time*, he always made sure to fit the image his potential clients expected.

You never get a second chance to make a good first impression. That's an old saying, but it's been repeated for generations because it is so right. In sales, making a good first impression is vital and it goes beyond your dress, make up, jewelry, speech and body language. Everything about you should fit what your buyer expects for the situation at hand.

You've Rehearsed the Part, Now Perform It

You can write, produce, direct, and star in your own movie and become a better salesperson at the same time. Start up your computer camera or use your smart phone. Turn it on, shout *"lights, camera, and action,"* and record yourself giving your presentation.

Forget all about camera angles, zooms and pans, art direction, music, titles, and all that. Just concentrate on the script and the performance. Get someone to play the role of buyer or client. If no one is available, don't hesitate to put on a one-man/woman show. Face the camera (and your own fears, eh?)

as if it were the potential future client and see how you look through someone else's eyes.

After you've wrapped the shoot, study the finished product. How was your:

- speaking voice

- posture

- body language

- eye contact

- dress, jewelry, overall appearance

- script

- approach

- presentation

- close

When reviewing your work, ask if you would buy something from this person. Then ask why or why not. Don't hold back. Be a harsh critic. After all, this is one movie you can start over from scratch until you're completely happy with both the script and the actor.

What you learn from this strategy might surprise you. Yes, you'll be lousy in some unexpected part of your presentation, but you'll also find a couple of areas where you're better than you thought. And after you review your movie and make the appropriate script changes, continue rehearsals until you see a positive difference. You want to deliver excellent content as smoothly as possible. When you reach that point, you'll be delivering star-quality performances from the approach in Act I all the way to the successful close of Act III.

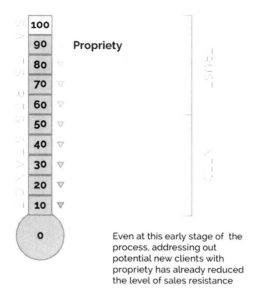

Even at this early stage of the process, addressing out potential new clients with propriety has already reduced the level of sales resistance

 ## Breaking the Dress Code

We've already discussed the bankers and farmers of the world. What about everyone in between? A good rule of thumb is to dress the way the people you want to sell to dress. What clothing will make those folks comfortable around you? Think about your buyer's comfort zone and go there.

Here are a few other tips.

Men shouldn't go overboard with jewelry. In most fields, anything more than a wedding ring, college ring, and watch will be considered flashy. Propriety, however, should always rule. If you're selling costume jewelry and presenting to the wardrobe manager for *"Mafia—The Musical,"* bedecking yourself with your golden trinkets may be entirely appropriate.

Women can wear more jewelry, but should also avoid that "flashy" look. Your new four-inch, solid silver ear fobs may be beautiful and worth a small fortune, but they'll get in the way of the sale if the sun reflecting off that shiny surface causes your client a bad case of retina burn.

Makeup for men should be limited to television or stage appearances and then it should only be applied by people who really know what they're doing. (Again, unless doing makeup is your business.)

Makeup for women is entirely appropriate. Err on the side of trendy, but conservative. Wearing no make-up at all could be a distraction and may paint you as someone who is not very conscientious about details.

Slim briefcases are vastly preferable to backpacks and wheeled carts (again, unless you're toting a supply of heavy samples). Don't be seen with a ragged or ratty briefcase in your hands. It will be taken as a symbol of how well you take care of business. Also, beware of setting your standard type of briefcase on a potential client's desk or conference table. You don't want to risk leaving a scratch or mark on them. That's not the type impression you're after at all. Also, the act of opening the standard hinged briefcase instantly builds a wall (the briefcase top) between you and the potential client. If you carry this type of case, open it on a chair or the floor. Avoid putting visual blocks between you and the client.

Always carry a very good quality pen and pencil. Our farmer will be used to getting his hands dirty, but he still doesn't want ink stains as a reward for approving a $75,000 purchase order.

Regardless of the dress code, always arrive neat and clean. Give yourself a quick once-over before meeting any client. Knowing you look great is a confidence builder.

Punctuality is a Plus

Barring those infamous Acts of God that appear in the clauses in your insurance papers, it is unforgivable for a salesperson to be late for any meeting with a potential client, whether it's in person, online, or over the phone. That's one of the many things you're constantly being judged on and a breach of that basic business etiquette is guaranteed to make a poor (and perhaps lasting) impression.

Punctuality requires careful time planning and that's good news because planning your time is simple and surprisingly easy. Here's proof and a way to instantly improve your efficiency by 20 percent or more with one simple habit.

Each evening, make a list of all the things you have to accomplish the following day. Rank them in the order of most important to least important. This little chore shouldn't take you more than a few minutes each evening. The next day instead of starting with the mental question of "Where do I begin?," all you have to do is follow your list.

The legendary TV and radio broadcaster, Earl Nightingale, was famous for using and teaching this strategy. Each evening, he would write out the six most important things he needed to do the next day, in order of importance, on a small card. That card then went into his shirt pocket. The next day, he would work on item #1 until it was finished before moving on to item #2. The list helped him concnetrate on what was truly important and greatly enhanced his ability to focus. Note: If you've never listened to Earl's extraordinary messages on success in business and in life, we highly recommend that you do.

Creating a to-do list in the evening allows your subconscious mind to start working on making those items happen even while you're sleeping. Try this technique. Give it enough time to prove itself, and you'll amaze your coworkers and clients at how quickly you accomplish your goals.

Step #2—Intent Statement

Read this sentence carefully: *Here's where we show you two ways to reduce sales resistance.* (What you just read is an example of an intent statement.) An intent statement is designed to reduce sales resistance by accomplishing two very important tasks. These are:

1. To introduce the agenda, so your future client knows what's about to take place, and

2. To let your buyer know that it's okay to say *"no,"* in order to relieve any perceived pressure

Number one, letting your potential client know your agenda, allows them to get a look at the territory just ahead.

You know the training philosophy of *"tell 'em what you're going to tell 'em. Tell 'em and then tell 'em what you told 'em."* Well, this is the *"tell 'em what you're going to tell 'em part."*

You always feel more secure starting on a road trip when you have a road map, right? The intent statement is the road map you share with your buyers. That way, they can concentrate on your presentation rather than worrying about what's coming up next. It helps to reduce at least one of their fears: the fear of the unknown. It's your way of saying, *"Hey, there are no unpleasant bumps in the road so just sit back and enjoy the ride."*

Number two, letting your buyer know that it's okay to say *"no"* does not contradict the one-time closing concept. In fact, it relieves so much tension that it actually increases the chances they'll say yes.

Nothing goes quite so far in reducing sales resistance as letting your buyers know right up front that you're *"not about to apply any high-pressure sales techniques."* Just stating the simple, honest truth that your product or service *"may not be right for everyone"* removes a tremendous load of fear. You'll notice the buyers will physically relax. Their curiosity will be piqued because you're different from all the other salespeople they've encountered. And, because of that, you'll have gained their focused attention. Your intent statement is a perfect example of sales techniques at their best. Everybody wins.

It's important to reassure your buyers. Some sales leaders suggest that you actually tell your buyers that *"it's okay to say no."* We think that's going a bit far. It's okay to *imply* that it's okay to say no to your presentation, but we don't encourage you to actually say those words.

Some buyers are so skittish they'll use such an opportunity to walk away (or escape, as they see it) even when you, he, she or they realize the purchase is a sound and needed solution to their challenges. And you won't have a leg to stand on because *"You said it was okay to say 'no'."*

Impress your buyers and clients with your sincere desire to do what's in their best interests and the idea of saying no will stay just that—an idea.

Here's a special note for folks in financial services and related industries. Much of your presentation will naturally focus on education. You have to educate your buyers and clients on money, how money works, and on the benefits they'll receive by becoming money-wise through the products and services you provide. Note in your intent statement that you will be providing this important information during your presentation and that their questions will be answered. Such a simple statement will go a long way to squelching some of that fear of the unknown that crops up whenever money is discussed.

⚖ Don't Allow Curiosity
To Kill The Commitment

Do not confuse getting your buyer in an open and curious frame of mind through your intent statement with other statements designed to gain commitment. The intent statement isn't related to urgency statements such as "Break the Pack" or "Today Only" that we will address later in this book.

Urgency statements do not belong in this portion of your presentation.

Here is a good example of a well-presented intent statement.

Introduction: *"John and Mary, if you don't mind, let me explain how we will proceed today.*

First, I'll tell you about our company.

Then, to determine if we have something that will meet your needs, and to be as brief as possible, I would like to ask a few questions. That would be okay with you, wouldn't it? (Wait for their answer. Most of the time, it'll be "yes.")

Next, if we do have a strong solution for your needs, I'll show you the product and after that we'll discuss the details of what needs to happen in order for us to serve your needs in the most effective and efficient manner possible."

Summarize: *"Now, I represent my company and this fine product that is used successfully by many happy clients. However, I'm not a high-pressure salesperson. I just don't believe in it. And I realize my product isn't for everyone. It may or may not be for you. I just hope you'll keep an open mind and at the end of my presentation, you'll tell me if this product is right for you. Okay?"*

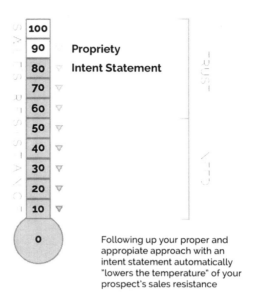

Following up your proper and appropiate approach with an intent statement automatically "lowers the temperature" of your prospect's sales resistance

The above example is most effective in a seller-initiated sales situation. It is often used when an incentive has been offered to the buyer for investing his or her time. A condensed version can be used in any sales situation after rapport has been established. Whatever the situation, letting your buyer know your intentions and to imply that it's okay to say no should be part of every intent statement.

Breathing Space

A one-time closing specialist always builds pauses and silences into the presentation. They allow the buyer time to consider important information, formulate appropriate questions, or just to catch his or her mental "breath." Authors do the same thing. So, we'll take a break now, let you absorb all the information you've just received, and then complete steps three, four and five to increasing trust in Chapter Six.

CHAPTER 6

Building trust from the buyer's
point of view is essential.

~Tom Hopkins

If we compare sales to an automobile
trip, then trust fuels the journey.

~Pat Leiby

The First Defense—Trust
Part II

As you will remember from early in Chapter Five, the five
steps to gaining trust are:

1. Propriety

2. Intent Statement

3. Commonality

4. Credibility

5. Competency

At this point, we're assuming you've gained a clear understanding of and made any necessary adjustments to your
personal grooming habits to meet each potential future client
with Propriety. We'll also assume you've mastered an effective Intent Statement so your potential client knows what the

agenda is and is relieved to know there's no pressure to own your product or service.

The last three steps to increasing trust, which continue to reduce sales resistance, are so important that they have their own title. We will identify them from here on simply as the *"Three Cs."*

Seek the All Too Uncommon Common Ground

Athletes, the really professional ones anyway, always warm up prior to a game, match or performance. They'll stretch, hop, skip, jump, and run through a few paces to get limber and loose for the upcoming event. Salespeople should run through a few paces with their potential clients just before the big event, too. Anyone who's been in sales for any length of time knows the value of this warm up. It's basic.

Of course, you don't have to make a friend to make a sale, but making an enemy won't move you any closer to that salesperson-of-the-month award.

People buy from people they like and trust. Finding common ground is an essential part of building relationships and you must do it early in the sales process. You can find common ground with anybody, any time, and any place if you'll just look hard enough. After all, you and your client are both human, right? Even during some of history's most tragic wars, bitter enemies found common ground.

Here's one famous example. During one of the most brutal battles of World War I, the fighting stopped one evening. It happened to be Christmas Eve. One side heard a Christmas carol floating on the cold air across the contested ground. The language was different, but everyone knew the tune and soon both sides were singing together. Before the evening was over those young men emerged from their muddy trenches, met in no man's land, and exchanged greetings and even humble Christmas gifts with their enemies.

If battle-hardened men who were in the midst of trying to conquer each other's territory can find common ground in no man's land, then certainly we salespeople can do the same thing on the showroom floor, at the executive desk, or the dining room table.

Step #3—Commonality

Finding that common ground is what step three is all about. During this early segment of the sales process you should search for areas of interest you share with this new person you've just met—your future client. The supply of topics is limitless. For example: the people they spend their non-working hours with, sports, hobbies, or current events are natural choices in consumer sales. If you're in business-to-business sales, you can always ask questions about their company or industry.

Because of the potential for highly-charged emotions, we recommend that you avoid seeking commonality in two areas: religion and politics, unless that's how you and your buyer met. For some people, there just is no common ground on these subjects. You either agree one hundred percent with their view or it's *"back to the trenches and fix the bayonets."* Those are battles you should choose not to fight because you can't win them.

In those rare cases where you just can't seem to find commonality, create some. Humor is an excellent tool for this purpose. Don't be afraid to use a light-hearted approach, especially if your buyer is showing signs of tension.

Here's an easy-going ice breaker for a visit with a couple: *"How did you two meet?"* Sometimes just the question itself will start a thaw. The answer to that question, for example, is almost always a humorous one. *"Oh, I picked her up in a bar. Ha-ha."* This would probably be followed by a mock-surprised, *"You did not!"* and a mild slap on the offending party's shoulder. Someone else might say *"Oh, he showed up at the back door and mom said I could keep him."*

Without realizing it, the customer has helped you break the ice and start the warm up. For example, the how-did-you-meet question often leads to brief comments about their dating and courtship. That friendly chatter usually brings up all kinds of warm feelings. The comfort level between salesperson and buyer grows right along with those feelings. They open up a part of their lives. Because you make the effort to find or build commonality, your customer opens up personal turf that few other salespeople ever see. With very little effort you're suddenly on the inside track like a friend of the family!

Never forget, buyers want to like you. They want to trust you. Do your part, and they'll likely do theirs and meet you halfway. When trust builds, sales resistance crumbles.

A Common Commonality Mistake

One of the most important things to remember during this early stage is to avoid asking sales questions.

We can't count the number of times we've observed or heard about inexperienced salespeople virtually attacking a potential client with sales questions the moment they enter the room. They come on like whirling dervishes—legs pumping, arms flailing, eyes wide and tongues wagging.

Would you want something like that coming your way? Neither does your potential client. So many sales have been blown to pieces before they ever had a chance to develop because the salesperson failed to develop commonality.

Think initially in terms of social and not sales situations. What type of conversation would you initiate at your friendly neighborhood sports pub, the church social, or in that shared cab ride from the airport? What follows are some examples of some ice-breaker questions to use with consumers.

"Are you from around here?"

"That's an exquisite brooch. Is it an heirloom?"

"Did you catch the game last night?" Choose the most predominant sport in your area.

A good way to open a conversation with executive level people who are more likely to want to get down to business would be to ask general questions about the organization.

"Isn't the pace of business today amazing?"

"Tell me a bit about how your company is doing this year."

"How long have you been with the company?"

None of those questions are inappropriate in the appropriate context. There's that propriety thing again.

Ask questions that will get your potential clients talking. At this point, you're not trying to close a sale. You're initiating a relationship. Listen to their answers and build your next question on those answers. That's all.

Time Creates Obligation

Have you ever met a stranger, become engaged in a conversation, and then discovered that somehow a significant amount of time had passed unnoticed? Sure, we all have. What happened was a bonding process in which two people found a common interest. The conversation and budding relationship quickly, easily, and naturally flowed out of that bond. People often say, *"You know, it feels like I've known you all my life"* after such a conversation, regardless of how brief.

How does that happen?

Well, in sales it happens because the salesperson makes it happen. The first step is to find a subject in which the other person is interested. Don't assume that just because you discover an area of particular interest, skill or knowledge that it's a subject they want to discuss. After all, the greatest chef in the world may just not want to get into the niceties of making sausage.

Look for something they want to talk about. For example, our chef may be the world's worst player on the golf course, but also an avid fan. As a salesperson, you'll do much better when you encourage a conversation about golf links with that person rather than the frying kind.

If you're familiar with the subject, golf for example, then you've made the connection. Proceed! If you don't know the difference between a tee and a green and green tea, you'd better move on to another topic.

Don't try to fake it here. The buyer will see right through it and you'll drive your chances of building common ground right into a self-made sand trap. Just keep politely asking questions on other topics. At some point, you and the buyer will find a shared common interest.

There is an excellent alternative to faking it, though. If your buyer seems especially interested in a topic that you are totally unfamiliar with, go for it. Admit your lack of knowledge and start asking questions. Get him or her talking up a storm about that fascinating subject.

As long as you are sincere, the other person will be flattered by your attention. Conversation will flow and commonality will be established. In fact, learning something new is one of the great benefits of earning a living in sales. Every day there's something different to encounter. How many occupations can boast that perk?

Here's the beauty of this situation. If your potential clients are reasonable people, all the time invested in talking about themselves and their interests creates an obligation on their part to listen to you when it is time to make your presentation. Human beings are wonderful that way. Respect and interest earns respect and interest.

Here are a few subjects to give you an idea of how building common ground can begin.

Job Related:

- *Tell me a bit about your job.*

- *Tell me what you do for a living.*

- *What's your occupation?*

- *What do you like most/least about your work?*

- *How long have you been doing this?*

- *What's the most interesting part of your job?*

- *What gives you the greatest amount of satisfaction at work?*

Child Related:

NOTE: Don't just jump into child-related questions until you see or receive a clue about the buyer's situation. You may be speaking with someone who is unable to have children, or who may have lost a child. You do not want to bring up any uncomfortable topics.

- *Do you have any children? How many?*

- *What are their names?*

- *How old are they?*

- *I bet you're proud of him/her/them.*

- *What interests are they developing?*

- *What do they do for fun?*

Family Related:

See the note above regarding child-related questions.

- *Are you married? (You might be meeting someone wearing gloves, okay?)*

- *Been married long?*

- *How many are in your family?*

- *Where do you folks live?*

- *Did you go on a honeymoon? Oh, where?*

- *Where does he/she work?*

- *What do you folks do for recreation?*

- *Do you share any hobbies?*

Location Related:

- *Are you from around here?*

- *Where are you from?*

- *What do you like most about living in your town?*

- *Have you traveled much?*

- *What is the most fun thing to do in your area?*

- *What would you recommend a tourist to see first?*

All of this information isn't gathered just to be discarded. You'll use much of it later when it comes time to cover your buyer's needs. We'll discuss that later in the book.

We could go on and on with this, but you get the idea. You want to be friendly and to encourage the other person to be friendly. Don't treat these questions as a checklist you have to march through like Sherman to the sea. Sure, General Sherman achieved his objective and shortened the Civil War, but he's still not too popular a figure down Georgia way. Your goal is conversation not conquest.

Also, avoid the trap of droning on about any given subject. Getting overly involved in a single topic of conversation will cut out valuable time you'll need for getting down to business and making your presentation. Just find the commonality. Establish it. Make sure your customer is comfortable with it. And at the appropriate moment, move on.

Speaking of moving in, let's see where all that common ground leads.

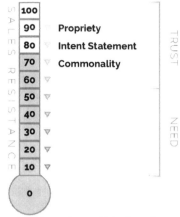

The trend continues. From a high of 100 degrees, your persistent and courteous efforts at propriety, your intent stamenent, and establishing commonality have reduced your customer's sa;es resistance down to 70 degrees and you're just getting started!

Step #4—Credibility

"Okay," you ask, *"now that I've established common ground, what do I do with it?"* The answer is *"move on."* And your destination is the next step, which is to prove your personal credibility to your customer.

The amount of time you invest establishing credibility varies according to a number of factors. Among these are:

- your product

- your product's required investment

- your industry

- your company

- you

- your buyer

- your buyer's level of need

- your buyer's budget

We could add *"etc."* or keep the list going for several pages, but you get the idea. Even a variable such as available time itself can have a dramatic effect. For example, you'll have a lot more seconds, minutes and hours in a flight from Dallas/Ft. Worth to Phoenix than in a four-floor ride in an elevator.

Of course, there are two key factors regarding time: (1) respect your customer's time, and (2) use it wisely.

Sharing a Timely Tale of Time Shares

The importance of credibility was proven rather dramatically years ago when the once-booming timeshare industry encountered some seriously bad times. A lot of those bad times were well-deserved. Poor personnel management, unscrupulous marketing practices, poor property management, and a "customer-be-darned" attitude took a heavy toll on profits and public relations.

Things were much worse than the implication in the title of the spaghetti western *"The Good, The Bad, and the Ugly."* The timeshares offered were either the good, the bad, or the *"I want my money back!"* As always, the good folks in the business got hammered right along with the bad. Things became so rough there was serious talk that the entire industry could collapse.

Fortunately, wise heads prevailed. Good management practices were established, serious self-regulation began, and some big name companies entered the field. Things began to change for the better and timeshares are now a well-respected, international, multi-billion dollar business with a new name, "fractional ownership."

What carried the industry through those rough times was the simple fact that the public liked the idea of vacation ownership and enjoyed the lifestyle it provided. Enough credibility had been built up to keep the concept alive during the dark days. A lot of very smart salespeople did everything they could to enhance that credibility. During this period of low sales, they provided forms of reinforcement to gain and hold the confidence of buyers.

These items included:

- documented articles from respected publications

- letters of endorsement

- referrals

- positive word of mouth

We chose timeshares to illustrate the point because good salespeople went to great lengths to prove credibility in every aspect of the business. That's something we admire and encourage you to emulate.

And we can almost hear your comments coming.

"Sure, but I sell furniture. We just don't have those kinds of problems."

"I'm an automobile salesperson. We've been in business more than half a century."

"My insurance company is one of the largest in the world."

"The appliances (jams and jellies or tires and tie-rods or pens and paper) in my store practically sell themselves."

True. Contrary to some of the comedians on television, a company or an industry may not be the true source of evil in our galaxy. However, you can still face a credibility challenge even if your product or company is a household name that can stand proudly on its own.

As a general rule, the salesperson is the unknown element. Personal relationships and referrals are exceptions, but in most cases customers won't automatically like and trust you because they just don't know you.

Yet.

Picture This

One of your authors was cursed (and blessed) with a rather young-looking face when he began his sales career. In fact, walk-in potential clients or people meeting him for the first time at his real estate office would say, *"Hi, sonny, is your dad around?"*

The trouble was, even though he certainly was credible, he didn't look credible to some prospects. Instead of resenting the situation or getting belligerent, he did something else. He overcame the challenge. He had a high quality portrait of himself taken with his wife and kids. This was displayed prominently on his desk so new arrivals could quickly see that *"sonny"* was indeed an established member of the community with a growing family. Over the years, that one picture eliminated hours of explanations and efforts to overcome a credibility issue.

You can use this same technique to picture yourself to your potential clients. Gather together information on your accomplishments as if you're creating an advertising flyer about yourself. You can do this on your computer or even with a careful hand, a pair of scissors, some glue and a clear plastic sleeve or two. Just pop in a couple of photographs of you and your family; you accepting that Woman of the Year Award; or anything that is appropriate. Include any appropriate business certifications, awards, or citations. Include any industry training you've taken or conventions you've attended where the latest knowledge was imparted.

Don't drop anything in as filler. Everything must build your professional reputation. The idea is to show your credibility. Don't try to recreate *"War and Peace"* or even *"War Cry"* comics. Include just enough material that you can present in no more than a few minutes to prove that you are the absolute best salesperson for that potential client to believe in.

You are, aren't you?

Then, be prepared to show it.

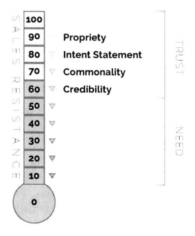

As your growing credibility lowers the temperature of sales resistance, the prospect of your one-time closing heat up.

Step #5—Competency

Visualize competency as a lump of clay. Unused it's nothing more than something sticking to the bottom of your shoes—useless, unappreciated and something that will just drag you down on a slow road to failure. Slapped between a couple of logs on a cabin it can protect you against the wind and rain and secure your shelter on a cold night. Formed into bricks it can become the building block of a skyscraper, a city, or even a civilization.

The question is what will you do with your allotment of clay?

Look at it from your client's point of view. When she wants, needs, or desires a product or service, how much time does she want to spend with an incompetent salesperson? The obvious answer is little or none. How much time do you think she'll invest with a competent one? That answer is just as obvious—all the time it takes.

Answer the following questions about yourself:

How competent are you at your work?

How well do you present your company's product or service?

Are you serving your company well?

Are you serving your clients well?

How good are you at discovering your potential clients' real needs?

Are you as good as you were last year? Better?

Are you working at peak performance right now?

Which is more important, your monthly quota or your buyers' challenges?

If any of these questions, or those most likely popping into your mind right now, are bringing up some feelings of doubt, then it's time to start working on building your competence.

Even if the answers have sent you into a spiraling depression, relax. There's good news. When you properly complete the first four steps of the trust segment of the one-time closing sales presentation, your potential client will perceive you to be competent. Looking competent isn't as vital as being competent, but it is important.

As Dr. Laurence J. Peter, author of the multimillion-copy-selling *"The Peter Principle"* and *"The Peter Prescription"* reminds us, *"Competence, like truth, beauty, and a contact lens, is in the eye of the beholder."* The buyers' eyes are going to be on you so make sure they see what they expect to see—a salesperson demonstrating a high level of competence.

The creation of that vision is all up to you. It's your job to make it a reality.

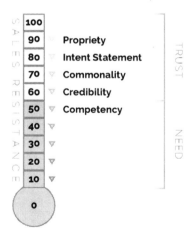

By taking the five steps to gaining trust one at a time and in proprer order you will soon reduce the sales resistance "temperature" by half and eliminate the NO TRUST hurdle!

The Three Cs—Just Do the Math

You can improve your odds of winning the numbers game of sales when you look at things through the eyes of your client. What does he or she really want and need from the process? *Your needs* are not irrelevant, but they should take second place to those you serve. Don't worry about your sales quota, your mortgage, or that long-awaited vacation in the Bahamas. Take care of your clients and the quotas. The bills, the vacations, and a lot more will take care of themselves.

It really boils down to a mathematical equation. A plus B always equals C. In this case, Three Cs.

Question Yourself

We do not mean to question your motives, your thoughts, or reasons for being in sales. We mean for you to put yourself in your client's mind and formulate a list of questions they might want to ask the salesperson—you. When you develop a good match, your potential clients feel that you are professional and credible—that you understand them. Competency is then automatic.

We're back to doing the math.

Propriety + Intent + Commonality + Credibility = Competency

Like all math equations, if the elements are correct and in the correct order, you always get the correct result. Numerous factors will dictate how you vary your questions.

Among them are:

- Is it a seller-initiated sale?

- Is it a buyer-initiated sale?

- Is there an investment range?

- What is the investment range?

- How much latitude do you have to negotiate the sale?

- What's going on in your industry?

- What are your company policies?

- How is the current economy affecting their business and yours?

- What is the projected economy and how will it affect this sale, if at all?

The key is to put yourself into the mind of your potential future client. What do buyers and clients really want to know?

If you're new to the profession of selling and find it challenging to develop your questions, ask a veteran salesperson to help you get started. As with any other skill, once you give it a couple of good tries, you'll learn, and eventually become a master.

Here are a couple of idea starters.

- How long have you/your company been in this business?

- What is the company all about?

- Can you provide me with recent testimonials?

- What kind of warranty do you provide?

- Tell me about service after the sale.

- Is there someone who can do the installation for me?

- How much does it cost?

- Are there a lot of colors available?

- What are the extras?

- When can I take ownership?

- When can I take possession?

You get the idea. The simplest way to draw up a list of questions is to think just like what you are when you're not selling—a consumer. What would you like to know before making your next purchase? (Commonality) Chances are that's pretty close to what your own customers are wondering. (Credibility)

Answer Before You're Asked

An excellent way to put your potential client at ease and begin building trust is to answer three or four of the most important questions right up front. Get them out of the way. This provides a measure of genuine relief for your potential clients.

"Whew, this isn't going to ruin my morning after all."

"Gosh, I didn't realize so many options were available."

"Gee, they're a lot more flexible on payment plans than I thought!"

You will answer the rest of the questions, and probably a couple you may not have considered yet, during the remainder of your presentation.

Most of the time your buyers will bring up questions that really aren't all that pertinent to the sale or very relevant to their real interest. It could be that they are nervous, trying to come up with better questions, or just stalling for time. It is your job to find and address the real questions.

One way to gauge the true importance of a question is to ignore it—once. Just respond with something like *"Good question. I'll address that specifically, later in my presentation, if that's okay with you."* Of course, it's okay. If the question is legitimate, you've told them you'll provide the answer. If you forget or don't cover it well enough, they can always bring it back up again. And if it's not relevant, then you can just forget it. Rarely will a customer restate an unimportant question. It just doesn't come back up because during your presentation you guide the process into more relevant areas.

Say Goodbye to B.R.I

Your enemies at this early stage of the sales process can be labeled B, R, and I. Those letters stand for:

- Boredom

- Resistance

- Impatience

These enemies can be dispatched quite early in the battle in order to serve your buyers well when you:

- establish the correct propriety

- deliver your intent statement

- ask casual warm-up questions for commonality

- show reasonable documentation of your credibility

- address and answer the Three Cs

When all of that has been done, you will have achieved competency and will have gained the level of trust necessary to continue with your presentation.

Once you have correctly used The Five Steps to Gaining Trust, your customer psychologically grants you their permission to continue. In fact, mentally they're encouraging you to get on with it. They're interested and even getting a bit excited about the prospect of owning the benefits of your product or service. That's a very good place for both of you to be. It's called a win/win situation.

Once you achieve the desired level of trust, your buyers will listen to you with a sense of respect and acceptance and you can say goodbye to boredom, resistance, and impatience.

The worst death of all is to be bored to death.

~Will Rogers

Now that we've said our goodbyes to BRI, let's move ahead and say hello to the next line of defense—your customer's need.

CHAPTER 7

Necessity is not an established
fact, but an interpretation.

~Frederick Wilhelm Nietzche

The Second Defense—Need
Part I

Nietzche got it right. A need is an interpretation.

- Your buyer doesn't really need a new car. He or she needs reliable transportation to get from place to place.

- She doesn't really want a new life insurance policy. She wants to leave something behind for her grandchildren.

- They say the company needs a new steam turbine for the power plant. You interpret that to mean they need greater efficiency, lower cost per kilowatt, happier customers, or higher fourth-quarter earnings.

Ralph Waldo Emerson said, *"The finest poems of the world have been expedients to get bread."* In other word's we do *this* to get *that*. It's all a matter of interpretation.

What Is *"That"*

We all know by now that the success of our sales presentations depends upon serving the needs of our customers. We also know that the entire sales process starts before we can possibly know those all-important needs.

In a way, it's like stepping into a large office building ready to make your presentation, but without knowing exactly where you're going. Is your appointment on the first floor or the fifty-first? Should you meet in the mezzanine, the coffee shop, or over at the security desk? Perhaps you should check in here at Acme, Inc. Or was it Ajax? Or Apex? You're surrounded by opportunity, but where precisely is this moment's opportunity?

Defining the illusive "that" is like finding the office directory on the first floor. Sometimes all you need is to get your bearings in order to get headed in the right direction.

No one should offer solutions to challenges not yet discovered or agreed upon. The one-call closing specialist begins the sales process from the first second of the initial meeting. Pros don't jump the gun and start offering solutions because he or she doesn't even know the challenges yet. They will instead initiate the discovery process. This process can be surprisingly brief or it can require a considerable investment of time. How much time depends upon who initiates the sale and the buyer's level of need.

For example a need can be:

- non-existent *("No thanks, I'm just looking.")*

- slight, but real *("No thanks, I'm just looking for a solution on my own."*

- real and immediate *("No thanks, I'm just looking for one of these.")*

- real and "help!" (*Yes thanks, I'm looking for ...*"—with sweat beads)

So, our goal is not only to determine the real challenge so we can offer a real solution, we also have to determine the level of that need.

Cold Reading Heats Up the Sale

Professional mind readers often use a technique called cold reading. It's a way of getting more information from a member of the audience than that audience member realizes they're giving.

It involves:

(1) asking questions, often in a shotgun approach, to get basic information;

(2) extreme active listening to pick up on the answers, body language, voice inflections, and other hidden bits and pieces of information; and

(3) feeding the information back to the audience in a way that surprises, excites, and entertains.

One-time closing salespeople do something similar to make certain they are serving the real needs of their clients.

When the potential client initiates the sale, there is some level of curiosity. Something brought these folks to your doorsteps or caused them to invite you to theirs. Often there is also an absolute level of need for your product or service. In these situations, the psychological sequence of events is much different from salesperson-initiated situations in which *we* start the process and entice potential clients with an offer of some type of incentive to speak or meet with us. When we first meet buyers, we must start the discovery and need process in a specific manner.

Do Not Put *Need* Before *Trust* in a Seller-Initiated Sale

We just mentioned something about jumping the gun. Putting discovering your buyers' need ahead of building sufficient trust is one of the most blatant and common examples of leaping over that firearm. Why is this basic mistake so common? Because it seems so natural, that's why.

The customer walks-in. He or she clearly has a need, a desire, and some kind of budget. They're ready to buy, aren't they? Surely, this is a prime example of a buyer-initiated sale with the buyer ready, willing, and able to be sold, right? Probably not. Without trust, you will never be able to close a sale. It just can't happen.

It is a mistake bordering on the criminal (or criminally insane) to attempt selling this way. You make several bad and often sale-destroying mistakes:

- You're desperate.

- You're just trying to make your quota.

- You don't care about their needs.

- You're already thinking about the next customer.

- You're under pressure from the sales manager to close sales now!

If you put need before trust you'll be taking a long hop, skip and jump off a short pier and will find yourself swimming in lost sales opportunities.

Take the Time to Read the Mind

And if you can't actually read minds, you can certainly (and rather easily) find out what's going on in there. The discovery process can begin as simply as saying, *"What brings you folks out to Ajax Autos today?"* Or, it can be as complex and time-invested (not "consuming") as having your buyer fill out a twenty-question survey. It all depends on the type of product you offer.

Many of the top companies we've trained in the health and fitness fields have built into the facility tours a questionnaire or survey that allows the health consultant to isolate the information necessary to find out what is *important, really important,* and *not very important at all* to the potential member. This valuable information is then used (or not, if it isn't important) to move the sale forward.

Whatever the situation, you must invest the time required to find out what is going on in your client's mind. You must take care of this important step completely before attempting to prescribe product benefits. There are no exceptions.

Take the real estate industry for example. A champion salesperson would never start showing property without first qualifying the potential buyer A significant number of variables will dictate which properties will and will not be shown.

For example:

- Family budget

- Expansions—babies on the way?

- Reductions—kids heading off to college?

- Neighborhoods

- Proximity to good schools

- Proximity to jobs for each spouse

- Location of major traffic arteries

- Distance to medical and health facilities

- Peace and quiet or "hubbub" of city life

Without qualifying, you'd be showing starter homes to millionaires and mansions to condo-seeking newlyweds. Initially, you have a lot of questions with big, long blanks where the answers should be. Begin with a friendly, conversational question such as, *"What brings you out to our store today?"* Generally, your customers will start filling in the blanks for you right way.

Read That Mind Back to Your Potential Client

Even as those blanks get filled in, you know there are other empty spaces on the page, so you keep asking those friendly questions. Slowly, surely and courteously you begin to narrow the focus on discovering their real needs. Additionally, your efforts are enhanced by your professionalism. People considering doing business with you appreciate your professional attitude. It proves you care. They'll respond positively because they'll begin to see that you are competent, credible, and trustworthy.

You see how this works? First things first. One step at a time. A place for everything, and everything in its place.

One of those steps is to repeat what you have just heard. This serves two very important purposes:

1. Repetition shows that you are actively listening to your buyer, and

2. It provides the opportunity for you and your customer to be clear in understanding each other.

128

Here are a few phrases to consider adding to your repertoire:

"Let me see if I understand."

"Let me show you an example so I can be sure I understand exactly what you want."

"If I'm hearing you correctly, you're looking for this, that and the other in blue, right?"

"So I discuss what is really important to you, Mrs. Buyer, let me see if I understand what you've just said."

The Benefits Of Reading The Body

There's another way to read someone's mind. It's called body language.

The study of body language has been around for a long time. Many of us have studied it. In fact, we consider it to be a "mini-science" of the profession of selling, just like dressing for success. These mini-sciences are important because, added together; they give you many more tools for becoming a highly-skilled professional.

You may already be aware of a few basic moves. However, most of us don't take advantage enough of this powerful and effective sales tool. We strongly recommend that you read one of today's popular books on this topic, or seek out the advice of body language professionals online such as on YouTube or TED Talks [www.ted.com/talks]. Once you study, observe, and begin to put body language theories into practice, you'll be delighted by how soon and how much you benefit.

Here are a few examples to illustrate our point:

Leaning forward typically means that your buyer is interested and is listening. Our experience has shown that when people are presented with new information, they begin that process with their backs pretty much against the backs of their chairs. When they begin to lean forward, this is a positive sign that they're ready for more. You should proceed with your presentation. You can even pick up the pace a bit.

Leaning back or glancing away is a clear sign that you are losing your buyer's interest. If this happens while you are in the middle of a long segment of your presentation, pause. Then summarize your last couple of points and ask a question to bring the buyer's focus back into the process. If you see this happening to a number of people in a group presentation, suggest a short break or initiate a question and answer session.

Crossed arms indicates doubt about what is being said. When this happens, proof is in order. Charts, graphs, diagrams, or testimonials are quite effective in overcoming doubt.

Just as it is important to "read" the other person's body language, it's important for the salesperson to send his or her own non-verbal signals. What you do can be as important and as effective as what you say.

Here are a few examples:

Sit positioned so you have good eye contact with all the people involved in the decision-making process. If you were with one person, you could sit by his or her side, but with more than one person, you want to be in a position to make good eye contact and observe any non-verbal communication between the buyers.

Use a pen or pointer to draw attention, at the appropriate time, to your visual aids. Notice how magicians use a magic wand to direct the attention for their audience to or from something. You can and should do the same thing. Do not be tentative or appear uncomfortable because that uncomfortable feeling will be transmitted directly to your buyer. Like a bad cold, it's catching.

Use open-hand gestures and eye contact. This shows that you are "open" and that you have nothing to hide. Be careful using the palm-out pushing gesture unless you're trying to eliminate a prospect's negative concern. Even then, push to the side and not directly toward your buyer.

These few examples give you a brief glance at an entire field of study. The more you study, observe, practice and apply, the more you will see just how powerful this tool is and how big a help it will be in your efforts to become a one-call closing specialist.

Don't Put Your Cart Before Your Horse Sense

Why should we put trust before need in a seller-initiated sale?

At some point during the sale, you will be required to ask important, often confidential, and sometimes very personal questions. Honest, 100% correct answers from your potential clients are essential to serving their real needs. Inaccurate answers are a waste of time for both parties and will only result in dissatisfaction for everyone concerned. Putting the cart before the horse creates a lose/lose situation.

You can't get valuable information about your customer's needs without trust.

Would you discuss your salary with someone you do not trust? Your plans for the future? Your family budget? Your heart condition? Your aging parent's medication needs?

Yet, these and other extremely serious and personal subjects come up all the time in sales. And, while they ought to come up, it should be only when appropriate. If they remain hidden in the background during the entire presentation, some salesperson has not built a foundation of trust and there will be no close. The reason for clients to hesitate to provide information, at least initially, is because the salesperson skipped the step of trust and jumped into a self-made mud puddle of need. (Now, the salesperson is in need—in need of a new buyer!)

Imagine an attractive young man approaching an attractive young woman at a singles get-together. What are his chances of building a relationship if he addresses her in the following manner?

HE: *"Excuse me, but I've been noticing you all evening."*

SHE: *"Oh?"*

HE: *"Oh, yes. That's a lovely dress. You must know a lot about fashion."*

SHE: *"Thank you. I enjoy paying attention to style."*

HE: *"Well, it certainly shows."*

SHE: *"And thank you again."*

HE: *"I think you are very attractive and I would like to ask you out to dinner..."*

SHE: *"You would?"*

HE: *"...but first would you mind telling me how old you are?"*

SHE: *"What?"*

HE: *"And how much you weigh?"*

SHE: *"What!"*

HE: *"Do you have any unusual medical conditions? Wait! Don't go! I have more questions for you!"*

We're certainly not romance experts, but we feel pretty safe in saying that young man has already seen the best moments of his new relationship. Suppose, however that the young woman was in a medical complex and the young man was her doctor.

"How old are you...How much do you weigh...Do you have any unusual medical conditions?" take on an entirely new context don't they? In fact, these questions seem completely appropriate. Instead of walking away, the young woman would probably provide the answers immediately and without question.

The difference is the level of trust.

A master at one-call closing gets accurate answers to such questions because he or she establishes trust with the buyer. Only then can the questions be answered with any degree of honesty. If you're going to be asking for a good bit of personal information, regarding debt or health matters, for example, you should always preface them with a phrase something like, *"I don't mean to be personal, but I can do a better job for you by getting the answers to these types of questions. Will that be okay?"* This is called getting permission to ask personal questions.

Here are a few examples of how to introduce the fact that you'll be asking personal questions:

"Not to be personal, but to do a better job for you, may I ask you a few questions?"

"To serve your needs to the best of my ability I need to know your specific situation and concerns. Do you mind if I ask you a few questions now?"

"With your permission, I'd like to ask a few questions. They will help me maximize your time here and make sure that I provide the right solution for your particular need. Okay?"

You see? It's not so difficult at all provided you put your buyer's needs first.

When you make the effort to prove that you, your product, and company are credible, and that your intentions are directed toward providing unique solutions to your clients' unique challenges, the discovery process becomes much easier. Sometimes it flows so naturally as to be unnoticeable as a sales step at all.

The Five Steps for Understanding and Developing Customer Needs

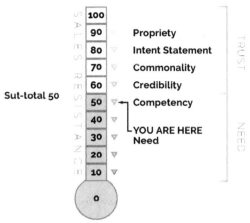

Pretend you're in a visit to Sales Wonderland and you're standing in front of a map of the complex. You've been so busy working your way through Sales Resistance Land that you've lost your place. Not to worry "You Are Here" halfway through. It's been great so far. And the ride's only half over!

Regardless of your product or service, regardless of your industry, your company, the economy, geographic location or any other factor, there are five basic steps you must take to develop and understand your potential client's real need. And remember, we are always talking about a buyer's real need. He doesn't want a four-on-the-floor Warthog XLF sports car. He wants to look good driving it. She doesn't want a bank loan. She wants to start her own business and call her own shots. They don't want a mortgage. They want to live together happily ever after, creating memories in their own home.

You can help buyers get there, wherever *"there"* may be, by following these steps:

1. Problem Identification*

2. Discovery

3. Qualify

4. Need Acknowledgement

5. Pact Acknowledgement

*NOTE: We are well aware that many of Tom's students will recognize the word *"problem"* as one taught never to say in front of clients. We are identifying a strategy here which, hopefully, you would never turn around and teach your client, so Tom gives his blessing to its use in this context.

Step #1—Problem Identification

What usually happens when a buyer enters a retail environment?

A salesperson rushes up with a big grin and a mighty *"May I help you?"* The salesperson, bless his or her heart, is trying to do the right thing. She wants to be polite, conscientious, and offer her services. Of course, this is usually followed by the equally mighty, *"No thanks. I'm just looking."*

The potential client has a number of reasons for this response. He, or she, might really just be looking. He might be killing time waiting for a movie at the other end of the mall, might be too shy to ask for help, or just not ready to divulge his vulnerability at this point. Maybe he just wants to take his time, set his own pace, and make his own decision whether or not to proceed.

We see two major challenges with the *"May I help you"* approach.

The first challenge is the *"may"* part. That automatically gives control of the situation to your prospect. We respect buyers. We need them and we want to serve them all the rest of our working lives, but we know they are not the most capable people to when it comes to going through the sales process.

The one-call closing specialist is far more qualified to see that each buyer gets precisely the product or service he or she needs. Why turn over the bus keys to someone who just stepped on board when you can *"leave the driving to us"* with a trained professional?

The second challenge concerns the word *"help."* Your friendly inquiry assumes and implies that your buyer is in need of help. Even people in desperate need are sometimes loath to admit it.

If you've ever seen reruns of Tim *"The Tool Man"* Taylor from television's *"Home Improvement,"* you'll realize that some folks are just incapable of admitting a need for help. They'd rather risk sawing Grandma's antique dinner table in half rather than admit to a lack of knowledge of saw blades.

Using the word *"help"* jumps you over a couple of important steps, as well. All you can expect from such a leap is a very hard landing. You'll be hearing *"May I help you—up"* from your less-than-impressed sales manager.

A much better opening statement would be. *"Hello. What brings you to Cox's Cabinet Corner?"*

Notice how this simple, friendly statement eliminates those two challenges. The prospect can't respond with a *"No"* or *"No, I'm just looking."* It's an open-ended question and any polite person will be obliged to provide a full answer. Two, you haven't put anyone on the defensive by implying they can't handle the something on their own.

In one sense, it's quite obvious why someone enters Cox's Cabinet Corner. They most likely want a cabinet. So why not jump directly to the close?

A one-time closing master knows there's more to the tale. Why does she want cabinets in the first place? How many cabinets does she need? What size? How many drawers? What finishes or colors? Glass or solid fronts? Modern or classical styles? Will they need cabinet liner paper? How about a set of brass cup hangers? Ah! You see, you don't know it all. That's what *problem identification* is all about.

YOU: *"Hello. What brings you to Cox's Cabinet Corner?"*

SHE: *"Oh, I'd like to unpack my fine china, but we need more room."*

YOU: *"So, you'd like something distinctive to display your fine china. Right?"*

SHE: *"Oh, yes. Can you show me something in a dark wood?"*

YOU: *"Of course. If you'll step over here. If you don't mind my asking, in what style is your home decorated..."*

At this point, the *problem* has been identified. Our salesperson has taken the appropriate step at the appropriate time. We gained insight into the buyer's situation by not leap-frogging ahead of them.

In some situations, problem identification can be a bit more complex, especially in seller-initiated sales. The need for exact measurements for certain home improvements, conducting water purity tests, property measurements, or surveys for vacation preferences are a few examples. But the principle remains the same. You must identify the problem before you can solve it.

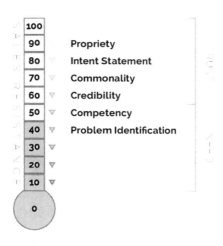

100	
90	Propriety
80	Intent Statement
70	Commonality
60	Credibility
50	Competency
40	Problem Identification
30	
20	
10	
0	

Your progress continues and things begin to get noticeably
easier as sales resistance continues to decline

Let's consider a few more examples of Problem Identification openings and the likely responses.

~"*Good morning. What brings you folks out to Ajax Autos today?*"

"*Well, the boy is headed to college next month. He'll be needing some wheels.*"

~"*Good afternoon, sir. What brings you out on such a soggy day?*"

"*The soggy day. I need a new rain coat.*"

"*Looks like you got here just in time. If you'll step over here I'll be glad to...*"

~"*Hi, folks. What brings you into Plugged-In Circuits on a bright day like today?*"

"We're headed to the beach. You guys have any Bluetooth® speakers?"

"Yes, sir. In fact we have a line that is designed specifically for beach use."

~*"Hi, thanks for coming in. Would you like to just look around or is there something in particular you're looking for?"*

Admittedly, these approaches won't eliminate every *"No, I'm just looking,"* but they will whittle down those responses to a paltry few. Try them and see for yourself.

Step #2—Discovery

Once you have identified the initial challenge, now and only now can you proceed on to Step Two—Discovery.

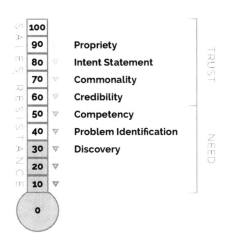

As inevitable as an equation, the five steps of need continue to lower sales resistance.

Once you have established the buyer's need and the buyer has acknowledged a need, the one-time closing specialist begins expanding that need. You want to increase your buyer's feeling of need for your product or service.

For example,

GREETING: *"Hi, folks what brings you to Royal Sound?"*

RESPONSE: *"We need a sound system for the office."*

DISCOVERY: *"Is this for just your personal office space or for the entire office building?"*

RESPONSE: *"We work out of our home."*

DISCOVERY: *"What type of system do you have in mind? We have   packaged units or we can custom design something for you from different products. Will you want video as well as audio? What will you be listening from? CDs? From an online music source? And would you like to run the system from your computers or phone. Or would you operate it as a stand-alone device?"*

Of course, there's a lot of time compression in that example, but you see what we mean. Place the preceding conversation in the context of your product or service. How would you begin expanding your customer's need? What type of questions could you ask? How could you develop appropriate follow up questions from their responses?

Asking these questions isn't rocket science, but it is a scientific approach. It's scientific in the sense that if you follow each step properly and in sequence you will get the desired answer. A + B = C. You can't get any more scientific than that.

Okay, we've covered the *"what."* Let's see *"why"* in our next step.

CHAPTER 8

The Second Defense—Need
Part II

Millions of sales have been lost because salespeople did not invest the time to qualify a potential client before choosing a product to present. Millions of hours have been wasted on sales that could never be for the same reason. You have to know whether or not your buyer needs and can afford your product or service.

Step #3—Qualify

"Do you folks have a price range in mind?"

That's the obvious question. And it's just as obvious that most people will be hesitant to jump into such an important area so early in the process. Asking too early will not only create barriers to open communication, such questions can actually offend your customer. It may actually increase sales resistance which is the opposite of what we're trying to accomplish in this step.

"Hmfff! What business is it of his our price range?"

Actually, their price range is your business, but asking about it should be handled with care.

For example, suppose you're working in a very upscale business when an unusual buyer walks in the front door. He's wearing a sweat-stained work shirt, blue jeans and muddy work boots. As they say out West, he looks like he was *"rode hard and put up wet."* Is this a likely buyer for your $25,000 round-the-world tour, your $175,000 luxury automobile or your or $1 million computer system?

Before you say, *"no,"* we'd like to ask, how do you know?

Tom Says: When I was a young salesperson, a man drove up to the office in a rather old car and got out. He wore tattered jeans and a work shirt. He was not groomed to any degree. He walked up to the front of the office and the other agents looked at me as if to say, "Oh, boy, this one's yours, Tom." They pre-judged the man and never made an attempt to get to know him.

His name was Bob Wyatt and he had just sold five gas stations and had millions of dollars to invest. I didn't know this at the time, but I treated him just as well as I did all my clients regardless of how much money they had.

Had I listened to my co-workers pre-judgments, I might not have treated him with the respect and courtesy everyone is due. He might have put up a defense right away and the relationship would never have gotten off the ground. Instead, we developed a great rapport. I worked hard for him for years and marketed quite a bit of real estate to him and for him. He turned out to be an excellent long-term and high-dollar client.

You can't judge a buyer by his clothing. Don't pre-judge!

You must qualify every buyer every time. Many of them will not be able to become clients. A one-call closing master weeds them out, takes steps necessary to keep in touch, and moves on. You always do this politely, of course. The man or woman you ignore or treat poorly today could easily be tomorrow's self-made millionaire, inherit a chunk of money, or win the lottery.

In some cases, the buyer really doesn't know his or her price range. They may be researching to find out how much things are. Qualifying will determine that information for both of you.

Take the Middle Ground to Get Out Of the Muddle Ground

Often buyers just don't have a clue as to a price range or how much they're willing to invest in a product or service. They may have a bottom line figure and even an over-the-top high figure, but no real concept of legitimate pricing for a particular product. Here's a technique guaranteed to help you establish how much they're willing to invest and to help them choose the next logical step in the process.

The Triplicate of Choice

The Triplicate of Choice is based on the fact that people prefer to make decisions based on choices. Rather than giving them a take-it-or-leave it, yes or no decision, you provide three different options.

You know going in that they will select only one of the three. Two out of the three are therefore wrong. So why not just approach them with that one amount, eh?

The answer is that you want to build in a comfort factor for your clients. You want to make the decision as easy as possible. Multiple choices make for faster and easier decisions.

145

And there's a bonus in that your potential client feels more in control of the situation.

Here's how the triplicate of choice strategy works: Begin with Amount #1 which should be twenty percent above what you are hoping they will invest. Use a statement something like this. *"Mr. Buyer, most of our happiest clients have been able to invest as much as $X for a quality hiking parka."* If I was hoping they would invest $200, the figure I would present would be $240.

Follow up with Amount #2 which should be between fifty percent and 100 percent above the amount you believe this person can invest. Say something along the lines of, *"We have those fortunate few who are able to invest as much as $300 for a hiking parka."*

Then offer Amount #3 which is the figure you want. Then say, *"Then, we have those folks on somewhat of a limited budget who can only invest about $200 for this type of gear."* This is the figure you want your customers to invest. Follow up with the statement *"Tell me, Mr. Buyer, which one of these people are you?"*

Now here is the fascinating part. Seventy percent of the time your buyers will choose the middle figure. They won't go for the high of $300 or even the low of $200, but seven out of ten times will choose the middle ground of $240—twenty percent above your expectation!

Now here is the fun part. Follow up immediately with a statement geared toward moving them from the $240 to the $200 figure. Why, you say, when they've already picked a higher, more profitable number? Because you want to serve your customer's interest, not make a fast buck. You can't serve your client if you don't close and here is a powerful means of moving to that one-call close. *"You know, right from the beginning I've felt we could save you some money, Mr. Prospect. I feel the two hundred dollar parka would be very right for your needs."*

Now what have we done? Lost forty dollars? Hardly. Using the Triplicate of Choice we've just removed a major objection that you could and probably would have heard later that *"it costs too much."*

That is how you serve your client and that is also how you close today and now.

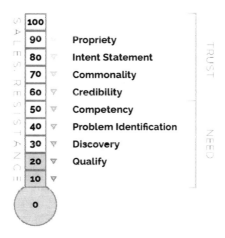

Taking the "middle road" lowers sales resistance and moves your closer to the one-time close by offering your customer real choices.

Step #4—Need Acknowledgement

Step #4 is primarily a summary of the preceding three steps leading to your buyer agreeing with your assessment of the situation. Once you have taken the NEED Steps #1, #2 and #3, executed them properly and in order, this step will provide a link that will help you close the sale at the appropriate time.

Here is an example of how it works.

YOU: *"So Mr. and Mrs. Buyer, let me see if I understand what you're seeking. You're looking for a 1/2 ton, four-wheel-drive pickup truck in the twenty-eight thousand dollar range. You want it to be no more than two years old and in a dark color, preferably blue or indigo. Is that correct?"*

THEM: *"Yes, that's exactly what we want."*

At this point, you and your potential buyers are in agreement. You're standing on common ground. This is a pivotal point in the sale. If the need has been acknowledged and agreed upon, you now have a green light to proceed with the sales process. It's time to move on.

By continuing to address the issues and to take the proper steps in proper order, your customer's sales resistance is rapidly approaching the zero point.

Step #5—Acknowledge the Pact

As the soon-to-be-fleeced Romans discovered one morning A.D. when the barbarians at the gate decided not to knock before entering, having a pact means very little unless both parties acknowledge it.

What is a pact?

A pact is an agreement made prior to the sales process. It is made with yourself, your spouse, significant other, or business associates. The typical pact is that you will NOT purchase anything during the process, today, right now, etc. We've all made them.

This is especially true in a seller-initiated sale and where the buyer may be offered a gift or incentive in return for listening to a presentation. We know we'll soon be feeling a sense of obligation, so we make a pact not to rush things or move ahead too quickly.

Many of your potential clients will initiate contact with you while having such a pact in force. The best way to handle these pacts is to address them head on, at the appropriate moment, of course.

A pact is likely to be formed any time there are two or more decision makers involved. Two areas especially prone to pacts are financial services and real estate. For example, if you're marketing financial services, you may be working with married couples. They'll typically make a pact that "whatever happens, we're not going to spend any money tonight."

In real estate, a buyer could call in response to a listing about a home. He or she could speak with a professional who uses proper telephone techniques to convince them to come in for a visit. When that person or persons come in you can just sense that they've made a pact. Even if you show them the perfect home in the perfect neighborhood and at the perfect investment, they've already decided not to make a purchase

149

now and you'll hear the old tried-and-true stalls of *"We have to think it over."* Or, *"We don't rush into things like this."*

Getting a Bounce

Step #5 is a bit like a bounce on a trampoline. As you come down you end a move, but at the same time and with the same effort you are beginning a new one and in sales, it is an on-ward and upward movement. This is the end of the discovery phase and the beginning of the help portion of the process.

Be aware that your customer is preparing for a sales *pitch* and we choose that word carefully. *Pitch* is what we refer to as a "nasty word" in sales. It's completely negative and it implies *"I am going to throw any old something at you"* or *"I just want your money."*

A much better, more professional word would be *"presen-tation"* or *"demonstration."* That's the language of a one-call closing specialist. But here we're working with buyers who are expecting the worst—a pitch. Your job is to turn that dreaded pitch into a welcome presentation.

Part of that process involves overcoming any pacts. Timing is critical. If you break the pact too early, you can create the very opposite effect of what you want. You can turn off your potential client and impede or even ruin the sale.

We believe in a two-step process to dissolve the power of the pact:

1. Acknowledge the pact

2. Break the pact.

In the first place, you may as well acknowledge a fact everyone already knows exists. Acknowledge the pact. This is best accomplished through the use of humor. Here's a good example.

> *"I bet you folks kicked off the covers this morning and said to each other, 'Honey, this is the day we are going to buy that big 'ol thingamabob, isn't that just great?'"*

Then wait for a response. In most cases, they will glance at each other, perhaps a bit sheepishly. They might even blush or smile.

At this point, you say, "You *didn't?*" with mock astonishment. Don't overdo it. You're not going for an Academy Award. Just stay loose and have fun with it. Make sure your buyers have fun, too.

Keep the humor flowing with, *"What really happened is that you probably made an agreement that 'no matter how good it sounds, we are NOT buying anything TODAY!' Am I right?"*

You'll get a shy *"yes"* or a couple of nods.

Keep going with, *"I completely understand your feelings because I have done the same thing myself."* This sometimes catches your client off guard. That's good. Suddenly they realize that you, like them, are a consumer. You're standing on common ground.

Follow up with, *"All I ask is that if you see something here today that would benefit you and your family and probably save some money in the process, that you don't let a little pact you both made earlier stand in your way. Fair enough?"*

Wow! That's strong. It's strong because it's honest. It's straightforward. It's logical and it keeps your clients' best interests in the forefront of your *presentation.* (Not your *"pitch."*)

You've now completed the ten steps in reducing sales resistance while developing trust and need. Step two, breaking the pact, will follow naturally in the sales acceptance portion of the process.

The graph shows that by following the process in the correct order you reduce sales resistance yo zero or at least to near zero. Now your customer is ready to listen to the remainder of your presentation.

Now, and only now, is the salesperson free (in the buyer's mind) to proceed into the actual sales process.

All We Need Now Is A Little Direction

At this point, we can begin directly addressing your potential client's wants, needs, and desires. By now, a sufficient level of trust should exist and, hopefully, you have, become a trusted advisor. You have achieved the goal of becoming liked, and trusted. Better still, your buyer has just recognized publicly that he or she has a specific need. And, you have all agreed on the need.

Sales resistance is at an all-time low. In fact, it is so low as to be non-existent. Of the four major obstacles you typically face, two have been overcome. To mix and mangle a few sports analogies, you're on the fifty yard line, you're at center court, and the bases are loaded. It's time for the offense to kick in to high gear and start running up some points.

At this point, it really doesn't matter whether the seller or the buyer initiated the sale. This is the point where your buyer is at last willing to listen to your presentation with curiosity and respect.

Please realize that the entire preceding process could take as little as ten to fifteen minutes—way less time that it has taken you to read to this point in the book. The timeframe required to get to this point will depend on who generated the sale and the type of product you offer.

You've earned the right to start selling now, so press on. That's where this book, your commitment, and your application of what you learn come in to play. The more you know and the better you are at what you do, the harder it is for the buyer to say *"no"* and the easier it is for them to say *"yes,"* if they're qualified. When you're good and when you have your buyer's best interest at heart, you have earned the right to this sale. Now, let's start building some sales acceptance!

Greater even than the greatest discovery is to keep open the way to future discovery.

~John Jacob Abel

CHAPTER 9

Help thy brother's boat across, and lo!
Thine own has reached the shore.

~Hindu Proverb

The Third Defense—Help

**All I Want Is Everything I Want Whenever I Want It. That's
All. Do you have a problem with that, buddy?**

Sorry. We're just trying to inject a little attitude into the discussion because there's a dominant attitude we salespeople
must confront all the time.

You may be the greatest salesperson in the world. Your
personality may sparkle. Words may flow off your golden
tongue like nectar from the gods of speech. You may care—really care—about each and every potential and satisfied client
as if they were long lost relatives.

Beyond that, your product or service may be the best there
is. Your reputation may be unblemished and your service af-
ter-the-sale record spotless. With all that backing you up, you
will still face the dominant customer attitude of *"What's in
it for me?"* They may use more polite language than that, but
that question is the ultimate bottom line.

You will face it at some point after you have gotten your
buyer to acknowledge that they have a definite need (the sub-

ject of our previous chapter). When that moment arrives, it's time to address that attitude because once buyers acknowledge they have a need requiring a solution, the one-time closing master has psychologically earned the right to start the sales acceptance process.

How, then, do we first-time closers answer, *"What's in it for me?"*

The Benefit of Facts

You address this attitude by quietly, logically, courteously, and relentlessly explaining your product's facts and benefits in such a way that the buyer envisions themselves enjoying its benefits.

Of course, this brings up an important topic, one that is too often ignored by too many salespeople—what exactly is a fact as it relates to my product or service?

- A fact is something that is real. It has a provable existence in that it can be seen, heard, touched, tasted, or smelled.

- A fact makes clear the obvious and the not so obvious. It is something that is undeniable and indisputable.

Occasionally someone's *perception* of a fact, as opposed to the actual and proven fact, can still have a powerful influence on a sale. Try selling a globe to a member of the Flat Earth Society! Of course, you can work with folks like this, too. *"Imagine, Mr. Buyer as you use this exquisite model of a round Earth (ha, ha, ha) to prove all those boneheads at NASA wrong."*

Most of the time a fact will be an accepted fact, or at least something to be considered. *"Does the Warthog 2000 really get 55 miles per gallon?"* These factually-based questions must be answered with factual answers. Of course, the Warthog 2000 gets 55 miles per gallon—stripped down to essential metal, running on a perfectly flat dry desert lake bed with a tail wind. That fact, of course is meaningless to your potential customers. They're concerned about real-world highway and city street figures. So, you'd better have those facts at hand.

Facts, regardless of how impressive, are not enough. Benefits are needed. A benefit is what the fact will do for your buyer. It answers the inevitable question, *"What's in it for me?"* The fact of a vehicle having high gas mileage means fewer trips to the pump and lower gasoline expenses.

When you are in this *help* portion of your presentation, the only statements you should make regarding your product or service should be facts and benefits. Anything else is extraneous and will only serve to distract your customer away from your presentation.

During the help phase of your presentation, the buyer begins to understand exactly what you and your company have to offer. This is also the point at which they begin to gain insight as to the benefits and advantages they will receive as an owner of your product or service.

Five Steps to Helping Your Buyer Make the Right Decision

When entering the benefits portion of your presentation, always show empathy with your buyers. Be wise enough to explain all the many ways the product will be of benefit based on the information you've already gathered about them starting way back in the commonality stage of things in chapter 6.

Having acknowledged the need, the buyers should realize that it is in their own best interests to listen to what you have to say. You are now an informed, respected, and trusted advisor. Your customers may not, and probably have not, made a decision to own your product or service, but they realize that you have their best interests at heart and your advice is informative and important.

We have defined five steps to helping your buyer. They are:

1. Product Identification

2. Company Experience

3. Salesperson Expertise

4. Third Party Endorsements

5. Product Features

Step #1—Product Identification

Regardless of the product, the state of the economy, the current demand, or any other factor, a one-time closing master always looks at every sale from the customer's point of view. For example, let's assume your company is Ajax Flooring and that it is a distinguished company with a long history. Your buyer arrives and is interested in new flooring for her whole house. The TV makeover shows have convinced her that it's time to update!

Fact: *"Mrs. Buyer, Ajax Flooring has been in the business of making our clients happy for over 30 years.*

Sounds good, doesn't it? But from the buyer's position, *"What's in it for me?"* A lot, really. The point is to say so in terms that appeal to the self-interest of the woman who's just entered your showroom.

Benefit: *"Since we've been installing floors longer than any other locally-owned company, our experience has allowed us to develop an installation system that* *speeds up the entire process. At the same time, we've incorporated all the options our buyers have told us they felt would add to the beauty of their homes. The result is a high-quality, yet quick-turnaround flooring package, customized for your needs. And our customers tell us, it's the most hassle-free experience they've ever had."*

Do you see the difference between the two statements? Both state the same basic facts, but the second is clearly more important to the buyer.

"Since Ajax Flooring has been serving local customers longer than any other company, we have developed an instinct for the features that are important to the people right here in this area. For example, we all know about how our climate affects certain types of surfaces. That's why we make sure every installation comes complete with six-month, one-year, and two-year checkups to ensure there's no deterioration of the flooring related to the installation. That saves you the hassle of filing a warranty claim if you do have any challenges."

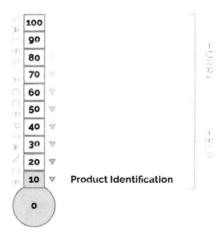

Once sales resistance is eliminated, you are still not ready to close the sale. You must begin building sales acceptance. Product identification is the first step.

In other examples, Mr. U.R. Elle isn't shopping for your Internet service. He needs to maintain customer satisfaction with instantaneous e-mail response to customer-service inquiries.

Miss Landsakes isn't really interested in the quality printing of her new real estate yard signs. She wants prospects to pick up the phone and call that phone number.

Mrs. Fuselage isn't really interested in ordering hydraulic aircraft controls. She wants a lower cost for maintenance and a smoother ride for her customers.

A helping word to one in trouble is often like a switch on a railroad track—an inch between wreck and smooth rolling prosperity.

~Henry Ward Beecher

Step #2—Company Experience

Your company's experience is important, but only in the context of a benefit or set of benefits to specific customers. Let's look at how you might present two opposite situations by thinking like a buyer and asking *"What's in it for me?"* First, let's take the case of a large, national retailer with outlets throughout the nation.

Fact: *"Apex MegaStore is America's largest retailer serving rural markets."*

Benefit: *"Our size and the large number of our outlets, lets us purchase in quantities far beyond our competition. That means we get lower prices, which we pass along to you folks. Also, we're located all around the country for* *your convenience, even when you're on a business trip or a vacation."*

Fact: *"One of the elements that has added to our growth is our 'no questions' philosophy with regard to returned items."*

Benefit: *"This has made our customers feel secure that they will always receive great value in any purchase made at Apex MegaStore."*

Now, let's apply the same philosophy to the opposite situation. Your store is a single-unit retail outlet.

Fact: *"The 'Lil Red Store has been serving this community from this same location for more than 25 years."*

That's great, but what's in it for your customer?

Benefit: *"Because our employees live locally, too, we have developed a unique insight into the specific needs of people in this area. We pay attention to what you're telling us you want and do our best to get the best quality merchandise for you. Naturally, the manufacturers we have chosen offer full warranties, so you can feel secure that you will always receive great value in any purchase made at The 'Lil Red Store."*

Regardless of your situation, you will always have facts that can be turned into benefits. Your goal as a one-call closing master is to present specific benefits targeted to specific needs or wants of specific buyers ... answering the question: *"What's in it for me?"*

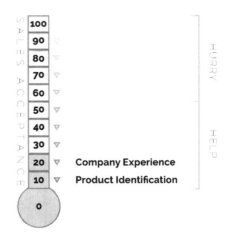

Nature abhors a vacuum and an empty space will always be occupied. By thinking like a customer and asking "what's in it for me" you begin filling the sales resistance space with sales acceptance.

Step #3—Salesperson Expertise

As a one-time closing salesperson, you have a tremendous value to offer buyers. But they'll never know unless you tell them. We draw a careful distinction between informing a potential client of your expertise and bragging. You may be the most knowledgeable person in your field, but unless you can make that fact relevant through benefits to your customer, you'll impress no one. In fact, you'll be **de**-pressing your opportunities to close the sale. Let's see how this works with an example from the timeshare industry.

Do not generalize. Show how you are *uniquely qualified* to help each individual achieve what he or she wants.

Fact: *"I grew up as an Army brat and later started my career in the military. I have traveled all over the world to many exotic places. While I was in the military,*

162

my job was bookkeeping and I was able to get a degree in accounting through a program offered by some top universities. After serving 20 years, my wife and I wanted to settle down in one place to raise our family, and still be able to travel on vacations as often as possible. I looked into many travel industry careers and timesharing made the most sense for me."

That was a good, brief statement of a career history and personal interests. Now let's apply that to the needs of your customer.

Benefit: *"My Army career and my travel experience have let me help my clients, and the people they refer to me, to take advantage of great opportunities to travel to unique locations around the globe and to enjoy those locations more like the locals do. It has also helped me become one of the top salespersons in my company. I feel it has been a win/win situation for my customers and me."*

The *"what's in it for me"* question is particularly relevant when you introduce a new element to your presentation. Is the new element significant to buyer needs or is it just something new for the sake of being new? Your personal history and qualifications are important, but realistically your buyer doesn't really care. The only way to make that person care is to present the facts in terms of benefits that make sense to their individual needs. So, even your own story should make the customers feel that out of all the salespeople in your business, you are the best to help them find a great solution to their needs.

Sales acceptance is inhanced when you show that of all the
salespeople in your business, you are the most qualified to
handle their need today, right now.

Step #4—Third Party Endorsements

When a new customer shows up at your door (website, show-room, catalog center, etc.) because someone recommended you, that's called a third party endorsement. They're one of the most powerful tools in a salesperson's arsenal. What makes them so strong is that the customer thinks of the referring party as an out-side expert, someone who is not directly involved with the sale.

A two-party story, the timeshare salesperson with the Army background, for example, may be strong, but it's not as powerful as a third party endorsement.

Tom says: This technique was particularly useful during my days of selling real estate. For example, when driving down the street showing a couple a number of potential new homes, I'd often see a previous buyer in front of the home I helped them acquire. It was so easy to make a point of stopping to say hello and asking how everything was going with the new home. Of course, the owners would smile and say how happy and excited they were in the house. That's a small act, but it built trust and confidence because the endorsement came from an impartial and uninvolved third party.

Even if you are the most honest, ethical, and straightforward salesperson in the world, your customer realizes that you have a financial interest in making the sale. And that's all right, but that fact does affect the customer's perceptions. Here's how a third party endorsement could work for our timesharing vet.

Fact: *"This brochure will show you some folks just like yourselves who have invested in timeshares from our company and how their experiences have improved their lives. Also, there's an article printed in CondoWorld Magazine about our unique ability to match people and places."*

All right, so you've been written up in the trade magazines. *"What's in it for me?"*

Benefit: *"What this means to you folks, is that we can create a timeshare plan that is a perfect match to your travel desires and your budget. As this article states, you'll see that our expertise means you'll get a lot more vacation for your vacation dollars."*

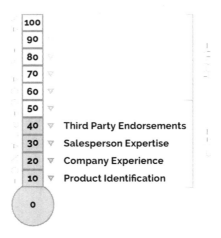

Notice how the negative space created when you eliminated all that sales resistance is filled up with the positive of sales acceptance.

Step #5—Product Features

At this point, the one-time closing master keeps the product features discussion to a more general nature. Save zeroing in on matching the specific product to the specific need for your product demonstration.

Here's a look through the subject of replacement windows from the buyer's viewpoint.

Fact: *"Our window units are made of the finest and highest grade aluminum money can buy. Then, they are coated with a baked-on enamel at the factory."*

Okay, that's good information. It's even interesting if you're shopping for replacement windows, but *"what's in it for me?"*

Benefit: *"Our construction techniques offer a number of money-saving benefits for you. For example, our clients find that they enjoy significant savings on heating bills and maintenance costs."*

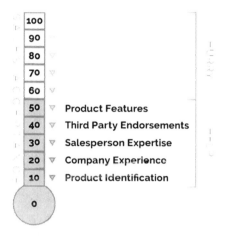

Product features are important, but at this tage in the process, keep your discussion of a general nature.

You see how this is done? A fact by itself is just that, a fact. Showing a direct correlation between that product feature and the needs or desires of your buyer turns it into a powerful benefit. Keep thinking like a buyer and the benefits keep on coming.

Benefit: *"This model is designed for the type of installation your home requires. In addition to the savings in energy costs, the exclusive tilt-in feature can save you time and effort when it comes time to clean your windows. That means less time scrubbing and more time enjoying the view through them."*

Copping an Attitude

When a customer has, at last, acknowledged a challenge and a need for a solution, you have earned the right to continue your presentation. The best way to continue is to cop your own attitude and we mean that in the most positive way possible.

Ask yourself, what is the attitude of your buyer? We don't mean the generic buyer, but the man, woman, family or committee across the desk. What is their attitude about you, your product, and your company? That information will prove invaluable in moving efficiently through your presentation to the one-time close.

The best way to find that attitude is to put yourself in your buyer's place and just ask, *"What's in it for me?"*

It is one of the most beautiful compensations in this life that no man can sincerely try to help another without helping himself.

~Ralph Waldo Emerson

Now is an excellent time to pause and reflect on that important truth.

CHAPTER 10

The Fourth Defense—Hurry
Part I

This is the heart of our one-time closing system, the core of **"Sell It Today, Sell It Now."** Every step, every phase of mastering one-time closing is important, but of all of them, mastering the step presented in this chapter is central to your success. This chapter is so important it could have been written first and all in bold face type, but like many salespeople do, we would have then been covering it out of sequence.

The Devil Made Me Do It!

The late comedian Flip Wilson developed a number of hilarious characters. One of them always refused to take personal responsibility for anything by saying *"the devil made me do it!"* That character has a lot in common with most buyers. At this stage of one-step closing, you will notice that your buyer has a strong desire to relieve himself or herself of all responsibility for the purchase. They are seeking, sometimes desperately, to say *"I didn't have any choice...I had to do it...I couldn't help myself."*

That kind of attitude can give you a devil of a time, but it's natural and it's all right provided you know how to handle that tricky little situation. When you master the techniques in this chapter, you will.

Send Back Your Be-Backs

A be-back is what happens when a potential client hears your presentation and then says something to the effect of *"I'll be back to talk things over tomorrow."* Like the old saying goes, far too frequently "tomorrow never comes." Most people would rather procrastinate. They'd prefer to sleep on it, think it over, kick it around for a while, and so on instead of making a decision now. This fact remains true even when the customer's need is high. There's just something about making a decision that intimidates some people. It's your job to help them over that hurdle.

A little thought about the psychology behind that kind of thinking makes things a bit more clear. People are taught from an early age to save their money, to avoid being a spendthrift, to hold onto their hard-earned cash. We must face the fact that there is a certain amount of guilt involved in spending money. That's an okay philosophy until it gets in the way of obtaining the goods and services you need. People often express this mentality with statements like the following.

> *"Yeah, the mechanic told me my car only had six months to live so I traded the old clunker in while I could still drive it into the dealership and get something for it."*

> *"I just had to have a new dress for the board presentation."*

> *"We had to have a bigger house so we could have some privacy from the kids, especially when all their friends come over."*

Do you see what's going on here? Those buyers are trying to relieve themselves of the responsibility for making a purchase. Some outside factor is forcing the situation. "The devil made me do it."

Hurry Up and Wait

Just like a waiter proud of his craft, you must be in a hurry to wait on the needs of your prospects and customers. You have to develop the mindset and the skills to structure your presentation so your buyer is relieved from the guilt of making a decision after the purchase.

Relieving your buyer of his or her purchasing guilt leads directly to more sales, more sales today, and more sales now.

This *"hurry"* part of the sales presentation is perfectly suited for this task. All you have to do is apply the information gathered during the *"need"* process, rely on the universal mindset of your buyer, and turn those be-backs into sales. That way the only time they'll be-back is when they'll be back for repeat business.

How to Turn Up the Heat of Sales Acceptance without Turning on High Pressure

The only thing high pressure can do is cause your buyer to blow his or her top. Two critical issues are involved.

1. Timing is essential. You must always know where you are in the presentation and how much time is left for you to complete it. Too often salespeople continue developing rapport and building trust long after those goals have been achieved. While you're still trying to make a friend, you become as welcome as the character in the Broadway play, *"The Man Who Wouldn't Leave."* Once you've achieved a goal in the sales process, move smoothly on to the next step. If you try to build your customer to 100 degrees of sales acceptance with a rapid boil of high pressure, you'll only succeed in making your presentation uncomfortable

or even offensive. Instead of heating things up, you'll just cool them down.

2. Working your way up to 100 degrees of sales acceptance must be done in small increments, one small step at a time. Steps of 10% or 20% at a time are ideal.

Let's take a closer look at how this is done.

The Three Reasons Customers Choose to Own Your Product or Service

People give all kinds of reasons for buying a product or service, but when you pin them down to *"seriously, now, why?"* the answers fall into one of three categories:

- Ownership solves a challenge they were having.

- Ownership satisfies a need.

- Owning this product or service is a goal aspired to.

Despite how it may be expressed, *"I wanted to surprise her...We just couldn't pass up a deal like that...He really had his heart set on it...We gave up on the old one before it gave up on us..."* and so on, every reason will fit nicely into the three listed above.

BUT, (and you knew that was coming, didn't you?) we one-time closers are concerned with something else. We want to make our presentations based on why people get involved today and why they take ownership now because that's when we want to close them—to get them involved. Customers go ahead *today* and now for another set of three reasons:

- They buy for need.

- They buy for desire.

- They buy for urgency.

We have already taken you through the need portion of the presentation. Now we'll show you how to create enough logical urgency to bring out the emotional power of desire. This logical process will also help you combat the inevitable onset of buyer's remorse all buyers feel. Buyer's remorse sets in the instant the purchase is made, the papers are approved, or the check changes hands. Immediately, the customer is filled with fear that he or she has done the wrong thing. *"I shouldn't have done that!" "I should've banked that money." "I spent too much." "Am I out of my mind?"* We one-call closers know this effect is coming and we prepare ourselves to help our buyers over this rough spot as we do with all the challenges throughout the sales process.

A Needed Word about Desire

There are two types of desire, also recognized as greed: inappropriate and appropriate. Inappropriate desire or greed was showcased in the film *"Wall Street"* in the character Gordon Gecko, played by Michael Douglas. Gecko made a lofty, noble-sounding speech to a group of stockholders on the subject of *"greed is goooood."* Of course, at the same time he was busy buying and breaking up companies, ruining businesses and destroying the lives of innocent working people. That's inappropriate desire. When a salesperson victimizes buyers by foisting some unwanted product on them, that's inappropriate.

Appropriate greed is what those shareholders thought Gecko meant in that speech. Appropriate greed is a legitimate desire to own a product or service. You want it and that's perfectly okay. Sales pros are there to help you get it!

173

Urgency Sales Acceptance

Hurry is the most important of your customer's four defenses. And, this section is the most important in mastering the art of the one-call close. Every previous step in the process has led to this one. It is time to create 100 degrees of sales acceptance without resorting to high-pressure sales tactics. Equally important, we'll show you how to do that without even creating the impression of using high-pressure sales.

Buyers can be a suspicious lot. You have to perform something like a high wire act in which you walk a fine line between pressuring your customers and serving them through a sense of urgency. Don't worry. As long as your heart is in the right place, with your customer's best interests, you'll do just fine.

The Sound System

The system we present here is a sound one and one that has been proven year after year. Somewhere out there some consciously competent salesperson is proving it right now. Our system is foolproof and that is no exaggeration. And because it is a system, anyone can use it. You don't need special talents, special skills or decades of experience. All you need is a desire to learn and to serve your potential clients.

Our system is based on two sound principles and they are infallible when it comes to working with a potential or existing client. We won't say you can't possibly go wrong, but to botch the presentation you'll have to work at it—really work at it.

Principle #1—Use the individual features of the product that the buyer is most interested in to create sales acceptance. Those are the reasons they will want to make the purchase now.

Principle #2—By using these individual features to create the necessary urgency a little at a time, your buyer will quite easily become a satisfied client. Ten or twenty degrees at a time, you will slowly "turn up the heat" until your buyer reaches 100 degrees of sales acceptance. He or she will go along with the process naturally and in a positive way.

So, how do we do that, you ask. Here's how:

The Five Steps to Hurry

The Five Steps to Hurry create a natural and positive sense of urgency:

1. **Product Demonstration** in which you showcase the features and benefits of your product as they relate to each buyer.

2. **Three-Option Close** for eliminating "I'd like to shop around" style objections.

3. **Break the Pact**, which was mentioned in an earlier chapter. Here you break up the agreement made by your buyers not to make a purchase today.

4. **Summary (Trial) Close** in which you summarize the key points of your presentation and test to see if the buyer is ready to consummate an agreement.

5. **Investment Close** during which the financial aspects are disclosed only after the salesperson is absolutely certain that theirs is the right product and it is the appropriate moment for the close.

We will address Steps #1 and #2 in this chapter and will finish the remaining three steps in Chapter Eleven.

Step #1—Product Demonstration

Make a solemn pledge to yourself, right now, that you will never make another product demonstration again without following this procedure. We're serious! Raise your hand, cross your heart and take the pledge. This is the system that will help turn you into a one-time closing champion.

The first step is to break down your product demonstration into segments highlighting each individual feature of your product or service that you know will benefit this individual client.

The second step is to present each of those features in the following manner, and only in the following manner.

State the FACT.

Show the BENEFIT.

Create URGENCY.

Ask for FEEDBACK.

Facts and benefits create the sale. Urgency and feedback make it happen now.

The first two, fact and benefit, are pretty easy. After all, the facts will be obvious or at least readily available with a little research. *"I recommend this property for immediate purchase because it is along the announced route of the new freeway."* Additionally, you should quite easily elaborate on specific benefits associated with those facts. *"This will make it more convenient for you to get wherever you need to go."* One will fall naturally and logically right after the other.

Urgency about each feature is something that the salesperson must create. It's not there until you make it so. It's not being pushy or trying to force your customer into a quick decision. Creating urgency requires effort and creativity to assure that your customer feels a genuine need to make a purchase

176

today and now. *"This means that you will double your investment within three years."*

Asking for feedback serves two purposes: it provides a way to monitor your progress and to see if your customer is ready for the next logical step.

Use the FACT-BENEFITS-URGENCY-FEEDBACK formula by breaking down the features of your specific product or service. To give you a better idea of how the process works, we will provide a number of examples using different products. Read them, study them, and imagine how the system will work with *your* product and *your* buyers.

You Auto Buy This

FACT: *"This powerful V-8 engine is the largest stock gasoline engine made in the U.S."*

This fact is obvious. You can simply lift the hood and show it. Even if the facts aren't that visual such as anti-lock brakes or a roadside assistance plan, for example, one of your product brochures will list them and more. Our point is that facts are easy to come by.

BENEFIT: *"This engine will allow you to pull your boat with ease and it's a standard feature with this model."*

To discover the appropriate benefit, just put yourself in your customer's mind and ask, *"What's in it for me?"* In this case, the buyer is concerned about the ease of pulling a boat from the house out to the lake. Power is obviously what's in it for him. Gas mileage, acceleration, braking, and turning ease could also be important benefits. After achieving trust and need, facts and benefits may do the selling, but urgency and feedback will do it now.

URGENCY: *"This particular engine will not be an option on next year's truck and even with the smaller engine there will be a higher sticker price on the new model. So next year you'd be paying more for the same model, but with less power."*

Without using any high pressure or being pushy, the salesperson has merely pointed out the significant advantage to making a purchase right now over procrastinating until later. Buying now is clearly in the customer's best interest according to the customer's own definition of need.

FEEDBACK: *"Because next year's model will look and ride exactly the same, which one do you think would fit your needs and pocket book the best?"*

The customer's answer will lead directly to the next appropriate step in the sales process.

Let's see how the system works on a few other products and services.

Pooling Your Efforts

Here's an example using a swimming pool in a resort property.

FACT: *"Here we have a full-sized pool, Jacuzzi and kiddie pool with an expansive deck."*

BENEFIT: *"As an owner here, you can relax by the heated pool any time of the year. We also have water aerobics, water volleyball, and many other activities for adults and children alike."*

URGENCY: *"This is our first pool. We have five others on the property. In fact, our developer is investing millions of dollars on additional amenities impacting the future* *value of the property and vacation lifestyle of our owners."*

FEEDBACK: *"At this point, I don't know if you are interested or not, but if this were something your family could use, when do you think would be the best time to get involved?"*

A Tablet Finds a New Owner

Our salesperson can give himself or herself a high five after using the system to turn a potential challenge into a reason to own.

FACT: *"This particular model has the latest technology."*

BENEFIT: *"Due to its high-speed processor and large memory, it will give you better picture and sound reproduction than anything else on the market when watching movies at the beach this summer."*

URGENCY: *"I have just two of these units in stock. One was returned because it was a gift and the person receiving it already had one. The package has been opened, but the unit has never been used. But because it's been opened, I can give it to you at a lower amount with the same guarantee as an unopened one."*

FEEDBACK: *"Although the unit is new and has never been used, or even plugged in, the carton was still opened. Technically, we can't sell it as new. Is having that carton opened something you can live with if it would save you money?"*

Lawn Down On the Job

Here our example is a lawn service.

FACT: *"I stopped by today to offer my services. You may have noticed that I mow and trim your neighbors' lawns across the street and next door."*

BENEFIT: *"Because I have a dozen customers in this neighborhood, as well as your next door neighbors, I can offer you a more economical fee than someone from across town. In addition, since I have to bring all my equipment each time, I can throw in trimming your shrubs at no extra charge."*

URGENCY: *"The flip side however, is that I can only handle two more accounts in this area because that will fill up my time on this side of town."*

FEEDBACK: *"I can have a quote prepared for you tomorrow or would Wednesday be better?"*

Clipping the Hedges

Use the preceding examples to spur some thought as to how the process will work with your product or service. We have seen how a fact, even something as simple as a swimming pool or the size of an engine, can be turned into a benefit to move the process toward a successful completion. We can use outside influences, such as other residential developments or an opened carton, to help us create the urgency necessary to close the sale now.

You should not, and must not, be perceived as someone using high-pressure sales tactics. Getting the proper feedback throughout the process is essential. If you wait until the time for the close to get feedback, your customer will start hedging on you. He or she will stall, back-peddle, and start making excuses for not making the purchase now. Something you said earlier in the presentation may have triggered a negative reaction. If you don't generate feedback throughout your presentation, you may never discover the concern(s) until it is too late to effectively address them. You have to clip these hedges when they first develop or they will grow out of control.

When you get proper feedback throughout your demonstration, your close becomes much easier because your buyer would be contradicting himself by refusing to go ahead. Your buyer is not an opponent to be worn down, but a patron to be helped. Even negative feedback is valuable because it lets you know where your buyer stands on a particular issue or feature.

Negative Feedback: *"Sure, the V-8 engine has a lot of power, but I bet it's a real gas guzzler."*

Positive Reaction: *"I'm glad you brought that up. Specifically because the V-8 engine is so powerful, it does not have to run beyond its capabilities when pulling a heavy load, such as your boat. A smaller engine has to work much harder and less efficiently to pull the same load. It actually uses more gasoline while towing."*

Without that negative feedback, this gas mileage issue could have remained dormant until the close when it would suddenly appear in the form of a major obstacle. Feedback, even the negative kind, provides you with golden opportunities to address important issues the moment the buyer thinks to bring them up, rather than after you have shown the investment and asked for the sale.

Make sure your presentation doesn't get clipped on the way to your one-time close. Product demonstration is basic. It's simple, but it's not as easy as falling off a log. You have to do your homework, study, and practice the techniques. You also need to research your client's real needs, wants, and concerns. Beyond that, you have to apply your own creative resources to put the entire sales presentation together in terms that provide the unique solution to your client's unique situation.

Combining customer research with your own creative abilities causes a natural reaction that raise the "temperature" of sales acceptance closer to the desired 100 degrees.

When you use the system properly, the math will astound you.

FACT + BENEFITS + URGENCY + FEEDBACK = SOLD TODAY, SOLD NOW

Repeat this mantra over and over, *"I will never give a product demonstration again without presenting the features in this manner:*

State the facts,

Show the benefits,

Create urgency and

Ask for feedback."

Step #2—The Three-Option Close

"Well, we'd like to look around a little more before we make a final decision."

"I'd like to take a look at a few more options before making a firm commitment."

"This is great, but we'd just like to see what else might be available."

"I would like to shop around first."

"Shop," "around" and *"more"* are three of the most dreaded words in sales. They form the basis of one of the biggest enemies of one-time closing, but there is an effective and proven way to overcome that most powerful of opponents. We call it the Three-Option Close. It works and it works really well because you use your buyer's own psychology to allow him/her/them to help you provide the unique product or service they really want and need.

This technique allows your buyers to do their "shopping around" *during* your presentation.

Here's how it works in four easy steps.

Step One: During the early stages of the hurry phase, you narrow down your prospect's need and price to a definable category or range. It's a standard part of every sales presentation. The further along the road you travel with your buyer, the better the picture you get of the ultimate destination.

Step Two: Review your product inventory and select three items that generally fit the parameters your customer has established. The items don't have to precisely match. Two of the three items can actually be outside those parameters, but they should be close.

For example, if your buyers are a young middle-class couple wanting a slightly larger house to make room for a family, you wouldn't show them that multi-million dollar mansion out on the lake. You wouldn't show them a tiny one-bedroom apartment either.

Three items are the optimum number to present. Fewer options don't offer enough choices and more options will tend to confuse the buyer.

We'll stay with that young couple throughout this example. One of the three homes you have selected will be the one you believe is the ideal home for their needs. Do not show this best option first. Show them the two comparable homes first and then wrap up with the ideal selection as your last presentation.

Let's suppose that the three comparable houses you have selected are priced at $185,000, $205,000 and $225,000. Which one would you show first? Your best option is to start with the lowest priced house, even if you think they'll choose a higher priced model—especially if you think they'll choose the higher priced model. The $185,000 home will not meet their expectations or standards and that's exactly the reaction you want. When you show them this home, introduce it by saying:

> *"Let me show you this particular home so that it will help me get a better idea of exactly the type of home you are looking for."*

After politely looking the place over and conferring silently among themselves, the couple will usually respond:

> *"This is nice, but we're really looking for something a bit nicer. We can afford a little more."*

Take a moment to look at the operative words in that nice win/win situation your customer just described. You as a sales person can earn more because you will be providing your customer with something nicer. Everybody wins.

Next, skip over the middle range house and go directly to that $225,000 unit. Again, they'll probably be impressed and will like it. But as it is at the extreme top of their budget or more likely just outside of their range, they'll respond with something along the lines of:

"This is really nice, but we just can't afford that price."

Now the process is nearing completion, but you don't slap your hands together, put a big grin on your face and say, *"Well, folks do I have a deal for you now!"* That smacks of high-pressure sales and ultimately the only one who gets smacked around is the salesperson. Agree that's what you thought, but that you needed to confirm they were still thinking along those lines. Then, phrase a response something close to this:

"There is another home I'd like to show you. After investing this time with you, and getting to know you and your needs a bit better, and getting your feedback on these other two properties, I think this model really might be just what you're looking for. It's got the features you want and it's within your price range. Let me check with the office to be sure it's still available."

Call in and then respond with, *"Yes, it's still on the market. It has all the features you want and at a reasonable $205,000. Would you like to see it?"*

Of course, they'd like to see it. That's why they're investing all this time with you. So, now you head out to see the home you had in mind all along. If this sounds a bit like manipulation, it isn't.

If you had taken your potential clients to the $205,000 house first, they still would have wanted to see more options. They would have a need to shop around some more, right? Well, by showing those other options you are giving them exactly what they want. The major difference with our system is that you allow your customers to do all their shopping around as part of your presentation.

Regardless of the amount, regardless of the product, every customer should leave the sale believing he, she, or they have gotten a bargain. Of course, you and your organization need to make a profit on each sale as well. Even if the customer is making an investment at the listed price, your presentation can stress how much value the customers are getting so they still feel as if they are getting that bargain. Sometimes an added gift will accomplish the same thing. The important point is that you want your customers walking away with the firm belief that they have gotten more than expected.

All you have done is helped prepare your buyer for a decision. More than that, you have helped prepare them for a positive decision now. As long as you are acting in good faith with the best interests of your clients at heart and are providing them a fair opportunity, you are not manipulating the situation or the people. You are just doing what you are supposed to do—helping that nice young family move into their dream home.

Ending a Driving Reign

Picture a young family in their mid-twenties with two young children. This husband is a hard-working carpenter earning a modest living. His wife is focused on raising their children and creating a picture perfect happy home. Their budget allows for one vehicle and that's a small truck. The husband must use it to travel from job to job across the community. His wife is beginning to show signs of cabin fever. A second car would put an end to the fever and would certainly make her chores significantly easier. They have even discussed acceptable makes and models, features and options, and even colors. Fortunately, they are due an income tax return which, combined with some of their savings, will get them into a "new" used car. The check and the savings total $9,000. They can't afford a penny more and certainly no additional monthly payments.

One day our carpenter gets rained out of a job. On the way home, he decides to drop into a local automobile dealership to kill a little time and to see if there just might be a good bargain available. As he steps out of his truck and under the large metal canopy over the cars he notices a salesman leaning on the hood of a car. The man smiles and nods. He looks as if he believes he is the king of the car lot, reigning supreme over all he surveys. He is the *"pitch man,"* the *"answer man,"* *"the man with the plan,"* and the giver and taker of all good *"deals."* He continues leaning on the hood of the car. When the carpenter approaches, the salesman asks, *"May I help you?"*

Our hard working young carpenter gives an overview of his family's needs and the parameters he and his wife have discussed. At last the king speaks. His voice is as boisterous as his over the top manner.

"Well, heh heh, my friend this is your lucky day. Why here's the little gem you are looking for right here. Go ahead, kick the tires, slam the doors, why it even still has a bit of that good old 'new car' smell. This is exactly what you are looking for."

Ask yourself a serious question. What has this salesman done to earn the carpenter's business? Has he really listened to his needs? Has he tried to provide a unique solution to a unique challenge? Has he put his buyer's interests first? Has he helped prepare his buyer to make a financial decision?

Certainly not and he'll probably record the incident as another no sale. *"The guy just wasn't ready to buy,"* he'll say. Well, our carpenter wasn't ready to buy because he wasn't prepared to make a purchase. Get that? He wasn't *prepared* by his salesperson to make a purchase.

Putting a Customer in the Driver's Seat

Let's look at the same situation, only this time our salesperson doesn't view herself as the absolute ruler of the car lot.

187

Instead, she believes she actually works for the buyer. Our carpenter drives into the lot. The young saleswoman approaches.

"Hi, my name is Mickey, what brings you by to see us today," she asks.

Charlie discusses the situation and lays out all the parameters of the purchase that he and his wife have discussed. Mickey then tries a much different approach than the "king."

"Charlie, if you don't mind I'd like to show you a couple of cars just to get a better idea of what you're looking for. Is that okay with you?"

"No problem. I'm just shopping around, though."

Mickey escorts her customer to a very nice car which, in a general way, fits the parameters they have just discussed.

"Nice car. How much does it cost," asks Charlie.

"It's in the twelve thousand dollar range. I'd have to check the price list to get the precise figure."

"Don't bother. There's no point. As I said, we can afford nine thousand and that's it."

"Okay, Charlie, let me show you something over here."

She takes him to look at a car that has obviously seen better days, much better days.

One look tells Charlie this isn't the car for his family.

"This isn't really what I'm looking for. I don't want my wife and kids riding around in something that might fall apart any second."

Mickey nods knowingly, but says, *"Well, it's only five thousand dollars."*

"Yes, but I told you I can afford nine thousand," he says. *"I need something a little better than this."*

At this point, Mickey looks a bit disappointed and with sincerity says, *"Well, Charlie, if I had a lot of gems like the one you're looking for I could sell a hundred a day. They are hard to come by."*

Charlie now believes that the sales process is winding down to an unsuccessful completion.

They start walking through the lot back toward his truck. After a couple of minutes, Mickey says, *"I was just thinking, Charlie..."*

"Yes?"

"We took in a trade last night that might just fit the bill. It has not been priced yet, but I would guess it will hit the lot at around ninety-five hundred."

"Yeah, but as I said..."

"Before you say no, let me explain something to you."

"Okay."

"First of all, the good news is that it is in great shape and has low mileage. I took my son out for ice cream in it last night just to check it out. It runs like a top."

"And the bad news?"

"Well, Charlie, the man who drove it last didn't much care about how the car looked. I don't think he ever waxed it at all. It also needs a new spare."

Charlie's interest perks up. Now he is aware that a positive offering might just be coming his way.

"The car is scheduled to go into our shop," says Mickey. *"It's slated for detailing and a new spare. If it goes into the shop, they'll charge the sales department at least four hundred dollars for a good clean up and a spare. The reason I'm telling you this is, if you were willing to do the clean-up yourself and get your own spare tire, we might be able to get the price down to where it fits your budget. Would you like to see it?"*

At this point Mickey walks right over to the car she was standing by when Charlie drove in. It's the same car as in the earlier scenario, but this time a one-time closing specialist is on the job. We have a different story, a different presentation, and a different conclusion. We have a sale.

The Three-Option Close is one of the most powerful ever used as Mickey has just proven. She was professional. She listened. She prepared her buyer for making a decision. And she created a situation that allowed Charlie to do all his shopping around during her presentation. If the car is even close to what his wife wants, Charlie is going to give serious consideration to making a purchase today and now. He'll probably pull out his phone to make a call to say, *"Honey, guess what I found?"*

Our Three-Option Close increases sales acceptance with dramatic results and it gets you closer to a one-time closing right now. This is especially true for big-ticket items, but it will work equally well in all price ranges, even shoes, for example.

Finding the Shoe That Fits

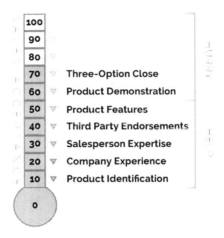

The Three-Option Close proves the old adage that "the third time's the charm!"

If you've ever paid attention to a presentation in a quality shoe store with a conscious competent, you will never see the salesperson come to the fitting part of the presentation with only one pair of shoes in hand. Being fully conscious and competent, he or she knows much better than that. Presenting just one pair of shoes forces your customer into the most restrictive of choices—*"yes"* or *"no."* We think you'll agree, that's not much of a choice. When the salesperson brings at least three pairs of shoes, the buyer's world of choices opens up.

The buyer can compare prices, colors, designs, materials, workmanship and so on. Not only does presenting choices increase your chance of closing today and now, it can also result in selling multiple pairs to your customer. *"I just can't make up my mind, so I'll just take 'em all!"*

With the Three-Option Close, you aren't limiting your customers to your selection. You are allowing them to make the purchase on their own. The technique will even work on items far less expensive than shoes.

"I can offer you a single roll of thread, a box of twelve, or this handy two-pack which saves you fifty cents. Which fits your needs best, Mrs. Prospect?"

Once you've created a situation in which your customer makes the desired choice, you still face a powerful obstacle. It's called The Pact. Breaking that pact and the other three steps to mastering the hurry step is discussed in Chapter Eleven.

CHAPTER 11

The Fourth Defense—Hurry
Part II

The Five Steps to the hurry phase of the sales process are:

1. Product Demonstration

2. Three-Option Close

3. Break the Pact

4. Summary (Trial) Close

5. Investment Close

We covered the first two stages in the previous chapter. Now let's continue where we left off with a way to address one of the most serious obstacles customers can place in your path.

Break the Pact

As you will remember, The Pact is an agreement between two or more decision-makers that they will not make any buying decisions that day.

"No matter what he says, Marge, we're not buying anything today, right?"

"That's right, Herbert, not today."

Their resolve can be anything from weak and tepid to mighty, indeed! Whatever the level of resistance, it is your duty to break that pact. As long as it remains in force, you cannot serve the best interests of these people—they won't let you. It's a curious, but true fact that one of the biggest obstacles preventing buyers from getting the goods and services they want and need is themselves. The old phrase that sometimes we're our own worst enemies is certainly true when it comes to The Pact.

Mickey has a Breakdown

Let's forget about Marge and Herbert for the time being and return to Charlie and Anna who have returned to Mickey's dealership to look at the car they can get for just $9000 plus a tire and a clean-up. During Mickey's presentation to the couple, she has discovered the existence of a pact. As we go through this example, mentally replace the cast with players drawn from your own experience and imagine yourself handling the situation with your own product.

After her presentation, Mickey asks, *"Anna, how do you like the car, overall?"* She then waits for a response.

Anna, remembering the pact, is non-committal. *"Oh, it's fine."*

Since the response is somewhat favorable, Mickey doesn't have to backtrack, repeat earlier points, or search for additional information. She continues. *"Charlie mentioned that his truck has a stick shift. How do you feel about the automatic transmission? Won't that make for easier driving when you're carrying a car load of kids, laundry, and groceries?"*

Since Mickey has been actively listening to everything Anna and Charlie have said, she already knows the answer. She selected the automatic transmission based on a positive comment Anna made earlier in the presentation. Of course, she'll give a positive response.

Mickey is carefully breaking down the pact, one decision-maker at a time.

The important thing at this point is to address each member of the pact as an individual. That holds true for a couple, a couple of business partners or a committee assigned to make a purchasing decision. Everyone plays an important role and must be sold individually.

Now, when Charlie hears Anna responding so positively, he thinks, *"Well, I'l l be. And she's the one who told me an hour ago we weren't going to buy anything today. I guess she's changed her mind."* He starts to think that their hardened position has softened. The pact weakens.

Mickey now turns to address Charlie. *"Do you feel that this car is something that fits your family's needs? Can you also see yourself using it, Charlie?"*

Again, she waits for a response and again she already has an excellent idea of what the answer will be. After all, Charlie called his wife, drove home to get her, and brought her all the way back to the dealership for that purpose.

"Well, it seems to be in good shape and you said it might fit our budget," he says.

Now Anna says to herself, *"Well, I'll be. And he's the one who told me an hour ago we weren't going to buy anything today. I guess he's changed his mind."*

Mickey is a great one-time closer. She addressed each member of the pact as an individual. In doing so, she has allowed each member to hear the other member make a positive statement about the purchase. There's a definite crack beginning to show in the solid structure of the pact.

In fact, at this point the pact has been broken. The second step regarding the pact has been accomplished. Now it's time for us to watch Mickey take the all-important final step.

Breaking the pact occurs in two stages. This is where you break the previously aknowledged pact.

The Summary Trial Close

The Summary Trial Close consists of two steps.

First, you summarize or review the main points of your presentation. This is not a long, drawn out recitation of facts and figures, fears and motivations. You just want to hit the highlights quickly, get an agreement, and move on.

Then, you go for a trial close.

Here's how Mickey would handle the situation.

"Anna and Charlie, let's go over what we have discussed here today, okay?"

"Okay."

Notice that Mickey mentioned Anna's name before Charlie's. It's not really essential in this sales situation, but as the car is for Anna's use, Mickey has chosen to address her first. This is just another example of a nuance of selling that can be critical to your success. Again, regardless of who the breadwinner or primary decision-maker might be, each person is important and must be recognized as such throughout your presentation.

Summary: *"Charlie, you told me that you'd like Anna to have a reliable car to go to the store and run errands during the day and not wait till you come home after work. Anna, you said you'd like to join a carpool for getting the kids to and from school rather than having them take the bus since they are on the early portion of the bus route. And Charlie, you said you'd feel better if you had back up transportation just in case you had a problem with your truck. Does that pretty well sum things up?"*

If you have covered all the important details, asked the appropriate questions, and listened well leading up to this point, their answer will be a solid *"yes"* which gives you permission to move on to the next step.

Trial Close: *"As we discussed, you both like this car and would use it daily if you owned it. That just leaves the money, doesn't it? But on the other hand, I don't want to assume something that is not the case, so I'd like to ask you a question. If the investment for this vehicle is right and affordable, is there any reason that would keep us from doing business, today?"*

That's strong! This statement or one similar to it, puts you right in the middle of the most critical part of your presentation. This is a make or break point and you must handle the next moments carefully or you can unravel all the work you've done up to this point.

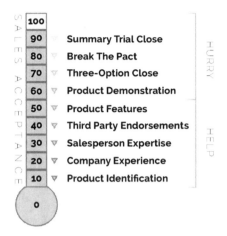

This is the most critical point of your sales presentation, the Summary Trial Close.

If your buyer gives you a negative response, you want it to show up before discussing the financial aspects of the sale. You do not want to get sidetracked answering objections after you have stated a figure. That type of distraction can disrupt your presentation and be fatal to a one-time close. Take your time. Be careful and attentive. Never move to the close until you are sure that your buyers are ready to make the trip with you.

If the buyer response is positive, continue on to the next step. That's the Investment Close.

If you encounter any resistance, handle it immediately. Do not allow that baggage to accompany you into the next phase of your trip.

At this point, your buyer should be anxious and excited to go over the investment details. If that is not the case, then something has gone awry. Don't worry. You can address whatever challenge may exist, provided you take a moment to discover it. It's probably something you missed earlier. Find it. Address it effectively and only then carry on.

Going ahead with the investment close, before they're ready, removes your leverage for the rest of the sales process.

And you'll need it.

The Investment Close (Discount)

Have you ever watched a sporting event when everything was going the way of one team or participant?

The quarterback was connecting with the long bombs.

The clean-up batter was hitting the pitches out of the park.

The ice skater was as graceful as a swan on a smooth alpine lake.

And then, without warning, the quarterback fumbles, the batter strikes out and the ice skater takes a spill and skids across the lake. Then everything shifts. The team or the player can't seem to regroup, recoup or get out of the soup. What has happened is a shift in momentum.

One single incident, often a minor one, has turned everything around and forced a move in the opposite direction. Undesirable consequences follow. Winners become losers or at best face a tremendous challenge in getting back up from where they've fallen.

That's why it's essential that you time your presentation so you are in the best possible closing posture when the final amount is given. You must maintain your leverage. If you are not in the correct position, assuredly you will drop the ball.

Take Your Best Shot, but Don't Shoot Yourself in the Foot

Research has proven time, and time again that once the amount has been given the majority of sales will occur within that specific meeting. The percentages drop off dramatically for any subsequent meetings, unless the type of product you market dictates a long sales process. To continue with sports imagery, you may have more than just one shot, but you will probably have only one **good** shot. Your best opportunity to make it is during the meeting when the money aspects are first disclosed.

Never, give the final investment until you have completed all the other steps correctly, and in the proper order, to place your buyer in a position to say "yes" if that amount is right.

If you cannot close at this point, you will experience a shift in momentum. And that shift will be *away from* your desired position. Your leverage gone, you'll be forced to endure a round of calls, follow-up calls, missed messages and perhaps missed opportunities.

"Hello, folks, heh heh, have you made that decision yet? Uh, you know someone else has shown an interest in that car you like so much, and, heh heh, I'd sure hate to see you lose it."

Of course, they can sense the fear in your voice. Desperation follow-ups like that diminish your chances of actually closing by a phenomenal degree. The buyer can hear the sweat beads popping out on your forehead. That's not exactly a way to build confidence, is it?

The Times are Not A-Changing

And neither are people. From the time the first cave man sold the second cave man the first used rock, through the time of Marco Polo wheeling and dealing with the fantastically wealthy merchants of the Far East, right on up to Gordon Gecko or Bill Gates and you and me—potential clients have always wanted to negotiate price. Nobody wants to pay the sticker price. Nobody wants to pay retail and nobody wants to pay the first amount they hear.

Smart merchants have always accepted the psychology of the human mind and have adjusted their investment structure to accommodate it. That's the way a one-time closing master adjusts to meet the needs of a potential client.

Special investments for special clients appear in as many varieties as there are products for those special people.

- Fire sales

- Closeouts

- Pre-construction sales

- Moving sales

- End of the year sales

- Holiday sales

- Christmas in July sales

- Boss on vacation sales

- Teachers-only back to school sales

The list could go on and on. Everyone responds differently and to different motivations, but the main point is that everybody responds to something. Sometimes, all it takes is a *"SALE"* sign to get someone motivated. Usually, however, some other factor is involved, such as:

- Solving a challenge

- Satisfying a need

- Reaching a goal

- Fulfilling a desire

- Meeting urgency

Understanding these reasons is important because people buy based on their emotions, but justify their purchases with the facts. A one-time closer works with both aspects during the sales process.

Some organizations have strict limits upon how much flexibility a salesperson can have during the sales process. You may have little real authority to make significant changes. If that is your system, then work the best you can within it.

Other companies allow great latitude regarding the investments and options. If you have the authority to determine the exact product and investment for your clients, or if you have significant input into that decision, we recommend that you use a two-step investment close.

> **Tom says:** *The definition of a close is: Professionally using a person's desire to own the benefits of your product and then blending your sincere desire to serve in helping a person make a decision that's truly **good for them**.*

Here's how it could work with Charlie and Anna.

INVESTMENT CLOSE #1

"Well, Charlie, Anna, there you have it. I can drop the amount down to $9200 if you'll take care of the spare yourself and if you don't care about the detailing. How does that sound?"

It won't sound quite right, of course, but Mickey already knows that.

"Well, Mickey, we appreciate it, but all we have is the nine thousand. That's not a negotiating tool. That's really all we have. Thanks, but we just have to pass."

Having gotten your customers so near the asking price should you press on and continue selling the virtues of the car even though they have said no? How about its clean engine? The large trunk space? The room for three kids in the back seat? Well, it doesn't really matter. Charlie and Anna have made it quite clear that the value of the car doesn't equal the amount they can pay. If you keep pushing, all you're likely to do is turn *"no"* into *"heck no!"* Or worse.

It's time to go to another option play.

With the Investment Close you will have reduced sales
resistance to zero, increased sales acceptance to the desired
100 degrees - and you have a sale!

INVESTMENT CLOSE #2

"I can see you'd really like this car. Let me see what I can do. Charlie, you're good with tools. There's a small dent in the top of the trunk, nothing serious. In fact, a quick bump with a rubber mallet should take care of it. But if we run it through the body shop, they'll charge for the time and labor. If I can use that to knock down the amount to a flat nine thousand, would that make you happy?"

Of course, it will. That's their price and you've just given them a lot of good reasons to justify the emotion they'll use in making the purchase.

Never offer a discount without justification. If you do you'll just lessen the credibility of your product or service. You'll lessen your own credibility, too. After all, if you could offer a discount like that why didn't you do so in the first place?

Offer the discount, but provide a logical reason. Mickey could just have easily offered another sound justification.

"Look, we have a new shipment of used cars coming in any day and we're about to be overstocked. I'll speak to my sales manager about meeting your number. I think he'll see the wisdom of making a sale now."

Justifying your discount allows your buyer to justify the purchase. *"Wow, did we get a great deal on this car. We just couldn't pass it up!"*

The two-step close differs from the three-option close in that it's not a product change. It's an investment change based on circumstances at hand, even if you have a hand in creating those circumstances. Introduced in conjunction with the Five Step Hurry portion, this is a very strong, extremely effective technique.

The Art Of The Long-Distance One-Time Close

A fairly common obstacle between the salesperson and the sale is the fact that the person or committee with the power to say *"yes"* is located across town, across the state or even across the globe. That obstacle isn't nearly as big as it was just a few years ago. In fact, thanks in large part to technology and people embracing it, in many cases this old challenge just doesn't matter anymore.

You can make successful presentations over long distances. Telephone and video conferencing are powerful tools that allow you to present and close regardless of distance.

Be aware, however, that certain strategies apply.

Often you can read body language through a video connection as well as in person, but even when you can't you can still hear voice inflections. You can tell fairly easily whether someone is paying attention by counting the length of pauses between their comments.

The excitement or lack of it, in their verbal responses such as "uh-huh" and "hmm" can speak volumes when you listen for them. Excitement or the lack of it is pretty easy to read. Of course, the person(s) on the other end of the line will be listening for your verbal clues, too.

If you want to make sure someone is 'on the same page' as you, just ask a question. Of course, you won't ask "are you guys paying attention?" Ask how something you've just covered relates to their business or ask their opinion of what you've just said. Just in case they really faded away, restate your last point or two to make sure they're up to speed.

You can also use the pregnant pause. Just pause for a few seconds. The silence will get the other folks wondering about what has happened. That brief moment of curiosity will bring their attention to what you'll say next and will help draw them back into your presentation.

Never forget that your product is the star of the show. That's especially true when you're making a long-distance presentation. If at all possible, have a sample or a strong visual of the product in the hands of the people on the other end of the line. You want them to see what you're speaking about.

When using a webcam affixed to your computer, other than yourself, what else will be showing on your buyer's screen? Do you really want them to see that dying plant you have on the shelf or the piles of unorganized books and papers on your desk? These are important considerations. Your potential clients will gather impressions about your competence from what they see.

The background to your videos should be simple. You can even put up a special background provided it is an attractive one. Be careful with plants. A tall fern placed improperly will appear to be growing out the top of your head and it's hard to make a serious point when you look a bit like the Jolly Green Giant on the screen.

To get a good idea of what to do, take a look at your local newscasts, the talking heads. Generally, your head and shoulders will fill the screen. Unless there's an overriding reason, a product demonstration for example, larger views are not necessary.

Like the newscasters, make friendly and confident eye contact with the camera. As the actors say, make the camera your friend. It's something like the speakers' technique of picking out one person in a large audience and occasionally addressing that one person directly in order to help make the presentation more personal. Be cautious about how much you look away from the camera to notes or other materials. Eye contact is even more important via video than in person.

If your presentation online requires slides or other visuals, maintain control of the flow. There are services that allow you to show a PowerPoint presentation on someone's computer while maintaining control through your own. Other services allow you to provide live audio and/or video of yourself while showing PowerPoint slides, websites or other video on the receiving computers. With a little careful planning, you can turn a long-distance presentation from a long shot into a sure thing.

That's it, folks. That's how you turn a seller-initiated selling situation in to a one-time closing situation. Now let's take a look at the other end of the spectrum, the buyer-initiated sale.

CHAPTER 12

To be trusted is a greater compliment than to be loved.

~George MacDonald

The Prospect-Initiated Sale

Take Care of the Hardest Chores First-A good rule of thumb is to always handle your most difficult chores first. That way, the longer you work, the easier the day becomes. It makes good sense. You tackle the most draining issues while you're fresh and at your peak of strength and energy. Later, as your energy levels dwindle, so does the level of energy required to take care of business.

That's what we have been doing in the previous chapters devoted to the seller-initiated sale. It's a more challenging subject to grasp than the buyer-initiated sale. As you will remember, the seller-initiated sale presents a number of situations requiring you to overcome the following:

- the no trust mindset

- the no need mindset

- the no help mindset

- the no hurry mindset

- an unknown company

- an unknown product

- an unknown salesperson

We've shown you how to handle, and handle well, each of these situations. Now that you've mastered them, it's time to move on to something a bit easier, but no less important. Since it's a more comfortable subject, let's slip into the prospect-initiated sale and see how it fits.

Going in Reverse is Not Backing Up

The prospect- or buyer-initiated sale is usually easier than the seller-initiated sale. It is also the more common of the two. Most of these types of sales are begun because a buyer walks into a showroom, makes a phone call, or logs onto a website. The salesperson is therefore responding to the buyer's needs right off the bat. Obviously, the buyer recognizes at least some level of need. There must also be some level of trust that provides the impetus for the buyer to initiate that call to you or your company over that of the competition.

Often, the potential client has already done a basic level of product and company research. In fact, it is common for the only unknown in the situation to be the salesperson. Some people just enjoy the act of shopping, but even these types who have a legitimate need will shy away from an establishment they do not trust.

A previous bad experience, poor word of mouth, even something as indefinable as a feeling of distrust can turn off most prospective buyers. This is why when the buyer initiates the sale we must reverse the first two obstacles in our list of four. Trust, need, help, and hurry become:

- Need

- Trust

- Help

● Hurry

Your first obstacle is no longer Trust. It is Need. Fortunately, this is not a case of *"no need."* Rather it is a case of *"some need."* Otherwise, that buyer wouldn't even be there with that nervous smile or questioning look on his or her face.

The same thing applies to the second obstacle, Trust. There must be at least some minimum level of trust for the buyer to make contact. That's why this situation is not as intense as the seller-initiated sale even for the same product or service. The salesperson is in a position where the job is to expand on the buyer's existing feelings rather than to attempt to create them.

For example, the discovery process of NEED is not as direct in a prospect-initiated sale as in a seller-initiated one. The discovery process isn't eliminated, but it is not nearly as in-depth or lengthy a process. When you ask, *"What brings you folks out to our store this evening,"* you will probably get a direct response. That response gives you a good idea, or at least a good clue, as to the reason for the visit. You're on your way into the sales process pretty quickly after the initial contact.

Here's an example.

YOU: *"Hi, folks what brings you out to Sofas Choice?"*

SHE: *"We need a new couch."*

(Problem Identification)

YOU: *"Did you have a particular color in mind? And would you be more interested in leather or fabric?"*

SHE: *"We were thinking of a medium brown in soft leather."*

(Discovery Expansion)

YOU: *"Do you have an approximate price range in mind?"*

SHE: *"Our neighbors purchased a nice one here for around $700."*

(Qualification)

YOU: *"Let me see if I understand exactly what you have in mind. You would like a soft leather couch, brown in color for around $700. Is that correct?"*

SHE: *"Exactly."*

(Need Acknowledgement)

YOU: *"Ma'am, what time frame do you have in mind? I have a reason for asking."*

SHE: *"Oh, we're not in any particular hurry. We'd like to shop around, you know. Why do you ask?"*

Okay, that's pretty straightforward and simple, isn't it? Your buyer arrived in a state of need. You then established and agreed upon a legitimate need and you've gathered a good bit of basic information. Now you are in a perfect position to enter and expand the *trust* portion of your presentation and then move on to the *help* and *hurry* segments.

You also realize that because your buyer took the initiative to approach your store, there is already some level of trust, too. Don't abuse it. That trust could be substantial, especially if it is due to the recommendation of a friend or relative. The trust could also be as frail as a butterfly's wing. Treat a buyer's trust with care and respect. Then, expand it.

The expansion is critical. Skip this step or rush it at your own peril. Any subject, concern, or area of the process that you bypass during your presentation will have a nasty habit of showing up when you need such an intrusion least. In other words, you'll take a long time to recover from any shortcut you take—if you can recover at all. You may have to be obvious. You may have to be subtle. It all depends upon your potential client and his or her need. Do whatever it takes in whatever ethical manner the situation requires.

Expanding trust will eliminate some *"be back"* situations and *"I have to shop around"* objections that might otherwise come up later in your presentation.

Let's return to Sofas Choice and see how that presentation is going.

Couch Your Words Carefully

SHE: *"Why do you ask?"*

YOU: *"Well, the sofa you're looking for is very popular. I've helped more happy clients own that particular sofa than any other in our store. In fact, I received a commendation from the manufacturer for being one of the top salespeople in the country for this particular sofa."*

SHE: *"You must sell a lot of them."*

YOU: *"I almost feel a little guilty because most of my business comes from customer referrals—like your neighbor. The quality of this sofa and the low maintenance of the leather make my job very easy."*

Has this salesperson (you) earned the trust of the buyer? You bet! Now, let's observe as you expand on that trust to include your store.

YOU: *"Sofas Choice just received a shipment of this particular sofa in a variety of colors. The manufacturer sent them to us on consignment because we are their largest dealer."*

What just happened here? You brought your company into the area of trust you already established with your potential client. More than that, you provided proof of your statement. Clearly, a major manufacturer would not offer such a large order on consignment if the company were not trustworthy. Always remember that a statement without proof is merely a claim in the mind of the customer. Proof turns statements into accepted reality.

Now you are poised to expand on *help* and *hurry*. These two pretty much follow the same pattern as in the seller-initiated sales process. The investment for the product or service will usually be the focus of your expansion.

> YOU: *"We received this particular shipment due to the fact that an order scheduled for shipment to a large apartment developer overseas was cancelled. Several major projects over there are on hold due to the economy. That's one of the reasons we can offer unusually low investments at this time for such a quality product."*
>
> SHE: *"That's good for me, right?"*
>
> YOU: *"Yes, ma'am."*
>
> SHE: *"Can you show me a couple of the models you mentioned?"*
>
> YOU: *"I would be very happy to. We are selling these quickly, as you can imagine. It is unusual to have an above-average product available at a below-average investment."*

That's how you expand on *help* for your buyer. And everything you do is for your buyer.

At this point, you'd escort her to the section of the store where the sofas you've been discussing are displayed. The process will continue there where she can see, feel, touch, and smell the product. This is where the concept of a new sofa begins to get real.

So far, you have effectively expanded on *need, trust,* and *help.* Now it's time to enter the *hurry* phase of the one-time close.

You will show your buyer several models to make sure she has a variety of options. You let her "shop around" during your presentation. Let's assume that she finds one in soft, brown leather just like the one she'd visualized before coming in to the store. There's a challenge, however. She really likes the fold-out sleeper model, but that unit is $300 more than she expected.

YOU: *"Well, Mary, how do you like this sofa? Isn't this just about what you were looking for?"*

SHE: *"Yes, it's perfect...except for the price. We could really use that sleeper feature, but it's just not worth the extra money."*

YOU: *"Well, unfortunately, that is the only brown, soft leather model we have left. I could order you one, but the investment would be just as high on the regular model."*

SHE: *"Why's that?"*

YOU: *"Our special offer is limited to the units from that overseas shipment I mentioned earlier. Actually, you would end up investing a little less for this one with the sleeper feature than if I ordered a standard model for you."*

SHE: *"I just don't know."*

YOU: *"If I may ask you a question, is it possible for you to transport this sofa yourself?"*

SHE: *"I guess it's possible. My friend, the one who bought her sofa here, has a van. I suppose we could borrow it."*

YOU: *"The reason I asked is that I could probably reduce the investment on this one by around one hundred dollars if we don't have to deliver it. And you'd get that sleeper feature. I don't believe you will find a better opportunity on this quality product anywhere. With a limited quantity of these models available, they'll sell out quickly."*

The sales process is sometimes like a roller coaster ride with lots of ups and downs, but in the hands of a competent one-time closing specialist, the ride gets smoothed out in the end. In this situation, our salesperson (you) has brought the buyer directly to a one-time closing point.

He (or she) has:

- used the tools provided (client, inventory, sales skills, etc.)

- expanded on need

- expanded on trust

- developed enough inventory knowledge to expand on help

- created a sense of urgency through hurry techniques

- avoided "be-back" and the "shop around" syndrome

- prepared the buyer to make a decision

A Suggestive Assumption

There are two types of closing that appear to be identical—*assumptive* selling and *suggestive* selling, but they are entirely different.

In *assumptive* selling, you speak as if your buyer already owns your product or service. For example,

"Mr. Smith, I know you'll feel true pride of ownership driving your new Gazelle 500 into your garage. Especially when you see the looks on your neighbor's faces." You'd never say, *"If you buy this Gazelle 500, Mr. Smith, I know you'll feel true pride of ownership..."*

In assumptive selling, you give your buyer ownership of the idea, product, or service to help move him or her toward making the correct decision to make the purchase.

In *suggestive* selling, as the name indicates, you suggest the sale. For example, when you order a big Double-Gulp Cola at your neighborhood ice cream parlor, your waitress might say, *"May I get you an apple turnover with that?"* She is suggesting an addition to the existing purchase, not assuming you will make one.

Both techniques can be effective in proper context, but do not make the mistake of assuming that they are the same.

Marching to the Same Tune Gets You to the Same Place at the Same Time

That place is a successful one-time close. The important thing is that you must march in step with your buyer regardless of who initiated the sale. You start out together, go through the process together, and arrive at the ultimate destination for a win/win successful journey. Never forget that the salesperson has the responsibility for finding the route and directing the course along the way.

You will have noticed some overlap in the tools and techniques of a seller-initiated sale and a prospect-initiated sale. Obviously, in this situation the process was more subtle and

217

spontaneous than a pre-arranged visit with a planned presentation. But the same philosophy was at work.

Align your presentation to the mindset and needs of your potential client and you'll both be celebrating a victory march at the end of the process, a victory in which everyone is the winner.

Here's a story that sums up all that we've learned so far.

Physician Heal Thyself

We think you'll relate to this story because at one time or another we've all visited a doctor. What happens when you're out of town and have an unexpected medical need? You ask for a referral, right? Let's suppose you're attending a one-time closing seminar and, suddenly, you feel a sharp pain where you ought not to be feeling sharp pains. All of a sudden, you have a serious case of "what the heck is that—ow!" The presentation you're hearing is intense, but the agony in your gut is even more intense. If you don't do something quickly, the only thing you'll get out of the seminar is a substantial bill from an ambulance company.

You get a referral to a local doctor from Tom or Pat. "Thanks," you say and you're on your way.

Moments later, you arrive at the medical arts building, find the office of Dr. Doman and enter. Right away you notice a few peculiarities in the dark and empty office. A small trashcan is overflowing with candy wrappers and miscellaneous papers which litter the floor. An office fern is a shade of brown you've never seen before. The little window into the back offices is made of stained glass, but you can't quite tell what made the stains. As the window squeaks open, a nurse greets you with a bland "What?" Her scrubs are wrinkled and in need of a wash. She is chewing gum and perhaps in need of a wash herself.

218

There is a definite lack of propriety in this office. But you don't leave. After all, this is a referral from Tom and Pat. You stay because you really are in need. The pain is getting worse.

As you try to balance the propriety against your need, you're considering stepping out into the hallway for a quick glance at the list of other doctors in the building, the recommended physician sticks his rather odd-shaped head into the waiting room. *"Moments very few will I waiting for you be,"* he says and he slams the door.

What kind of accent is that, you wonder. The little man sounded more like Yoda from *Star Wars* than anyone else. This guy might be the greatest doctor in the world, but how are you going to communicate? You are experiencing a serious lack of commonality. But, Tom and Pat referred the good doctor, so you stick around.

As the pain in your stomach increases, so does your discomfort in other areas. You notice the doctor's certificates mounted in cheap, plastic frames nailed to the wall at odd angles. Oh-oh. His name is Dr. Yodaman and he's a graduate of Dr. Feelgoods' School of Medicine and Taxidermy. It appears to be a franchise. Suddenly the mental balloon of credibility goes pop!

Your skin begins to turn pale and not just from the stomach pain. Realizing that discretion is the better part of pallor, you make a retreat to the lobby and check out the list of other doctors in the building. You notice a Dr. Domain. That must be who Tom and Pat meant.

The pain in your stomach sometimes causes you to bend over and support yourself against the hallway. You need help and fast so you enter the domain of...well, Dr. Domain.

Wow, what a difference! The office is clean and bright. The neat as a pin medical assistant greets you with a friendly smile. This, you think, is what a doctor's office should look like. You are experiencing the right propriety.

Dr. Domain politely escorts another patient out. He looks and sounds professional as he pauses to engage you in a brief, friendly conversation. He's just like one of those young professionals from the television show, *"Grey's Anatomy,"* you think. Now you are experiencing commonality.

Even the degree, expensively matted and framed, is from the Harvard Medical School. That's a lot of credibility right there. This doctor must have a higher degree of competence, too. While that ache in your stomach hasn't let up, the other painful concerns in your mind are going away rather quickly.

You are soon shown into the doctor's office. Before you can describe your ailments, he hands you a small capsule. *"Listen, it doesn't matter what's wrong with you,"* he says. *"I've invented a new medication that will cure anything from a broken leg to cancer and everything in between. Take this now and you'll be okay within twenty-four hours."*

Well! What's wrong with this picture? You have propriety, commonality, credibility, etc. Surely, he must be competent, except that he's prescribing something that is patently absurd. Even without a medical degree, you know there's no such thing as a magic cure-all.

Now, you're back in the lobby looking at that tenant list again. Ah! There's a Dr. Yo. That must be the one.

Fifteen minutes later, you are inside Dr. Yo's examining room. She, her medical assistant, and her office have passed all your concerns about commonality, credibility, etc., but you're still a bit wary.

She listens to your explanation for seeing her. She asks intelligent questions about pain levels, duration of pain, fluctuations, and other symptoms. Then she says, *"Here is how I think we should proceed. First, I'd like to take a blood sample and an X-ray. I'll look them over and meet with you in less than an hour. Okay?"* That's an intent statement which builds trust.

"Sure, let's get going," you say. This doctor seems to know her stuff...or at least her stomach aches.

An hour later, you meet again. She looks you in the eye, confidently and with care, and says, *"Well, the tests and our computer readouts agree. They confirm what I believed to be the issue."* This is her discovery agreement. *"At this point your issue is not serious,"* she says. *"In fact, there's a new medication which should take care of it within four hours."* She has just addressed your need for help. Even though your stomach still hurts, you're already feeling better.

Then she gets a serious look on her face. *"The down side is that if we don't treat you right now, I'll see you in surgery in twenty-four hours."* That's certainly an inducement to hurry.

This sale has definitely been closed.

Salesperson Heal Thyself

Doctors have a tremendous edge compared to salespeople. Doctors are usually perceived as competent until proven otherwise. Our society quite rightly places a high value and high level of esteem on people who practice the healing arts.

Unfortunately, some folks believe salespeople are practitioners of the stealing arts. We know that's an unfortunate and untrue belief. We have our share of scoundrels, just like every other industry, but for whatever reason we seem to pay a higher price (and we do mean 'price' here) for our bad apples than other industries.

Salespeople are often perceived as incompetent until they prove otherwise. The why of that is irrelevant. The important fact is that you must work with and overcome that inaccurate stereotype. It's there, so you have to deal with it.

As we have proven, you must break down the four defenses to make your case each and every time. There are only four obstacles in your way. As you are the healer of your own process, so to speak, it's your responsibility to heal yourself of this negative stereotype. Overcoming those four defenses so that you can truly serve the real needs of your clients is your duty as well as your job.

The key is simply asking yourself, *"Who initiated the sale?"* And then to prescribe the best medicine.

CHAPTER 13

Additional Methods for Increasing Your Proficiency Numbers

Combining needs is an extremely powerful one-time closing technique that is especially suited for overcoming the "other" factor. Here's a story that demonstrates the effectiveness of this technique.

Pat the Nice

Many years ago Pat, the appliance mechanic, was just starting out in life. He had a small family and an income to match. He was living with his mother-in-law who required minimal rent. Her generosity was much appreciated, but the family had a strong desire to move out and make it on their own.

One evening Eddy, the encyclopedia salesman, knocked on the door and initiated a sales presentation. He was dressed professionally, handled himself as a professional, and made a very good opening presentation. The young mechanic was even in those days interested in sales. So he let the Eddy in to deliver his presentation.

Eddy did a very good warm up and discovery, although Pat did an equally good job of thwarting his efforts. He explained that his young son was only weeks old. The boy couldn't even speak, much less read so there was just no need in the household for a set of encyclopedias.

The salesman was good at his job and soon discovered that the young mechanic had a special, personal goal. Pat wanted to build his own home and he even bragged about his capabilities as a handyman, and how his own sweat equity would save him a lot of money, enough for Pat and his family to get into that home a lot sooner than most folks would think.

Eddy was very good at his job. He quickly dropped the idea of educating Pat's son and switched tactics. He explained that if Pat invested in the encyclopedias he would be able to use the reference services offered by the encyclopedia company to improve his skills in carpentry, plumbing, electrical work, and other areas directly related to building that little dream house for his family. That concept made a lot of sense and all for just $19 a month. Back in those days, $19 was a lot of money for Pat, but in his mind the benefits far outweighed the cost. Pat invested in the set of encyclopedias.

Within 24 hours "buyer's remorse" set in. However, Pat didn't cancel the order. For a long time, he didn't think very kindly of Eddy—rationalizing that Eddy talked him into the purchase. Still he admired the man's strategy and the lesson stayed with him.

Pat the Nice—Part Two

Let's fast forward five years. Pat was a well-read appliance repairman, burnt out on his job. He decided that there was something more to life than lying under washing machines in dark and dirty basements. He applied to Metropolitan Life to become a salesperson, was hired, and assigned to a poor neighborhood in Akron, Ohio.

The first thing MET did was send Pat to school in Chicago for training in sales and insurance law. He was pumped up and ready to take on the world as MET's newest and most excited salesperson. The second phase of his training began when he was assigned to an experienced sales manager for a couple of weeks. This was to introduce him to the clients in his territory, continue his training, and to get some real-world experience under the guidance of a real pro.

Pat's first day involved collecting the premium for a whole life policy from a young woman with a new baby. He asked if she had insured the infant, yet. She said no and even volunteered that her husband wasn't insured either. Delighted, the manager set up an appointment for a return visit that evening. They returned as promised and discussed the benefits of additional coverage with the young woman and her husband. The sales manager laid out a program that would cover husband, wife, child, and any additional children for just $11 a month.

It was a good and fair offer, but when the sales manager moved to close the husband said he just wasn't interested. The change from friendly-and-open to "no thanks" and close-mouthed was abrupt and somewhat shocking. The sales manager became flustered and even a bit angered. He tried a number of tried-and-true closes without success. Not only did these tactics have no effect, they seemed to strengthen the young father's resolve. He even said he didn't believe in insurance companies, banks, or other institutions.

"What do you believe in," asked the sales manager.

"I believe in collecting coins," said the young man. "The only thing I use a bank for is a safety deposit box for my coins."

The situation kept its downward spiral, going from bad to worse to hopeless. Finally, the sales manager began packing his sales kit in preparation for leaving. At that moment, Pat remembered Eddy, the encyclopedia salesman. He asked if he could speak. The manager agreed.

Pat began questioning the young father about his coin collection. The man had been collecting since the age of sixteen, for approximately twelve years. As he continued talking about the collection, his entire demeanor changed. He became more open and friendly. It was easy to see that he was proud of his hobby and his level of achievement and expertise in it. Pat said that he knew nothing about collecting coins and wondered if the values rose and fell like the stock market. Did outside influences affect their value? The young collector replied that they did and spent the next few minutes discussing the coin collection, and how he attended various meets and exhibits.

Pat, waited for the appropriate moment, and asked, *"Since you have no insurance now and if, God forbid, something were to happen to you, your wife would have to go to that safety deposit box, remove enough coins to pay for your funeral and to have enough money to get by on for a while, right?"*

"I guess so," he said. Clearly, the troubling thought had never crossed his mind.

"If it happened at a time when the coins were down in value, could it possibly wipe out your twelve-year effort?"

Shocked, he readily agreed that it could happen just that way.

Pat continued. *"Other people insure their businesses. Wouldn't it make good sense to spend just a few dollars a month to protect your investment in your coin collection?"*

The young father paused, thought for just a few minutes and said, *"Write it up."*

Pat's sales manager was as elated as he was surprised.

By remembering Eddy the encyclopedia salesman, and his Combining Needs technique, and more importantly, by learning from him, Pat made the first of many, many one-time closes in a long and successful career. You can learn from the example of Pat and Eddy. Practice Combining Needs through a good discovery and adapting the *help* part of your presentation. By doing so, you will become more successful.

Shall We Dance?

This strategy is not for all products and services, but some situations call for a specialist to be brought in during the process specifically to get the final agreement. This is often called the *"turnover"* or T.O. close and it can be very effective when handled with care. Handled improperly, you'll just end up with two wallflowers instead of one while your buyer waltzes off to find another partner. These are important points when you have a third-party higher authority for the hand-off to help with the close.

Usually the decision to use the turnover close is made in advance by the sales manager. At the appropriate moment during the first salesperson's presentation, the specialist is brought in. Good timing is essential. If the hand-off occurs at an inappropriate moment, the buyers can become confused, and can even be turned off by the process.

For example, let's say the sales process consists of ten steps and the turnover is scheduled for step number nine. The first salesperson should carry the presentation on his or her own through step eight. The specialist arrives at step nine for the turnover and completes the process. If the specialist arrives at step ten, however, then step nine is missing, and the sale is lost. If the specialist arrives at step six there is an overlap. The buyer can become confused as to who is responsible for what and the sale is lost.

This moment of transition is critical. We call it *"the dance"* because it's such a strategic moment. The sales people, the sales managers, and the closing specialists must all be synchronized in absolute harmony. Like a dance, their movements must be graceful and timed perfectly. The turnover requires study, practice and role play to make the performance flawless.

When the turnover occurs, all aspects of the sale should have been addressed except the total amount and/or terms. The customer should be in a position to say *"yes now"* if the investment and terms are acceptable.

For instance, sometimes a potential client is embarrassed about his or her lack of ability to pay. If this fact isn't discovered until the close, your entire time invested in the presentation could be a wasted effort.

You must smoke out these and other concerns before offering any discounts or negotiating any other aspects of the sale. Otherwise, your customer will stick to his guns and refuse to make the purchase. He doesn't want to lose face and be embarrassed by admitting that the product or service is too expensive for his budget.

All these and other considerations must be addressed prior to making the turnover. That way the specialist only needs to know the pertinent information regarding your particular potential client.

The specialist must clearly understand the reason he or she is being brought to the table and the specific reason the customer is giving for not buying today. Once the turnover is made, the first salesperson should be absolutely quiet and allow the specialist to do his or her job. If there is a need for him to speak, the specialist should give a non-verbal cue.

The turnover is a wonderful technique when it is truly needed. Every once in a while, we need a partner because, like the song says, sometimes it takes two to tango.

Words Fail Me...

Often a potential client is unfamiliar with a product or service and the company providing it. This is especially true in one-time closing situations and particularly so in seldom-purchased products. You may be the best salesperson in the world, your ethics beyond dispute, and your motives dedicated 100 percent to serving the needs of your customer. Still, in this scenario, it's best for you to use third party influences to establish the Trust, Need, and Hurry necessary to achieve a one-time close.

Too often a salesperson will use himself or herself as a second party influencer in an attempt to help close the buyer. *"I use this product myself and I can tell you from personal experience, it's really great."* That's fine, but that strategy can only take you so far. After all, even if you're absolutely correct, you're still a prejudiced party in the buyer's mind. Of course, you think the product is the best thing since sliced bread. You sell the darn things! You can't blame the buyer for a little bit of incredulity. Using yourself as a reference can backfire if you paint your word pictures in terms that sound improbable (even if they're true).

Realize that you will be working with wary customers and that sometimes your words just aren't enough. You need third party influencers to beef up your credibility so you can close today and now.

Pictures Don't Lie

If you can't dash out and grab the nearest third party influencers, at least you can use their experiences. Using testimonials, preferably video testimonials or at least the written word with photos, are an excellent way of having third parties speak on your behalf.

Since your buyer lacks experience with your product, your company, and even you, it's a terrific idea to graphically show some of the successful experiences your other happy clients have experienced. Well-known third parties can be very influential, as you've seen with the many celebrity endorsements of products in infomercials. Your customer thinks, *"Well if she uses the stuff, it must be good."* Well-known people don't have to be celebrities of world renown. They can be folks around town who are probably known or at least known of by your buyer.

> *"Principle A. Cheever down at the high school purchased one last year and he's amazed at how well it works."*

> *"Minnie Vann, over at the mayor's office says she doesn't know how she ever got along without one."*

That's a third party influence. It's a good idea to have a lot of third party information on hand and then select one closest to the profile of your buyer.

You can even spread your third party influencers throughout your presentation. Have one for trust, one for need, one each for help and hurry. Don't have them available just in case. Design them right into your presentation. Consider which influence works best with what step. Does Minnie Vann's testimonial fit best with *need* or with *help*? Give it some thought and then put her testimonial to work in the right place.

Often a buyer will attempt to throw you off your presentation by jumping ahead. *"Yeah, yeah, yeah. Just tell me the price, okay?"* There's a similar danger when a buyer lures you into using a third party influencer in a portion of your presentation when you'd planned on using it in another. Our advice is to stick to your game plan and don't allow anything, even the buyer you are serving, throw you off.

And You Can Make Book on That!

Presentation books (PowerPoint presentations or videos) are great sales aids when put together with care, organization, attention to detail and with the potential needs of your buyers in mind.

Poorly planned and executed, they can destroy your credibility. If the presentation book is dog-eared, uses third or fourth generation copies, or is randomly organized, all that reflects poorly on you, your product, and your company.

If you have to fumble around looking for the relevant material or if you have to interrupt your presentation to pick up fallen bits of paper, you're about to be a very lonely and disappointed salesperson. Your buyer is bound to think, *"If his presentation is that sloppy, just think how bad their product must be!"* This is not the kind of impression you want to make with your potential clients.

On the other hand, a well-organized, concise, relevant, crisp, and clean presentation "speaks" volumes about your professionalism and the high quality of your product and service. When it comes to effective presentations, you should, as a friend in the entertainment industry says, *"book it!"*

Fifteen Keys to Handling Objections

Handling objections is one of the greatest fears of the inexperienced salesperson and that's simply because they do not yet understand the tremendous help objections can be to closing sales.

Here are 15 keys to help readjust your attitude toward what is potentially one of your greatest assets in any sale.

Key #1: If they're not interested enough to offer objections, they're not interested in buying. Objections are a good measure of how much real thought is behind the purchase and just how serious your buyer may or may not be. An objection is nothing more than a request for information. That's all.

Key #2: Plan on handling objections in every presentation. They're like rungs on the ladder, just another step in a process leading to success. Don't ever leave out this essential aspect of selling. Don't leave it to chance. Prepare for it with all the other necessary steps.

Key #3: There are two kinds of objections: minor and major. Minor objections are nothing more than a defense mechanism. Your customer probably just wants to slow down the sales process a bit. He or she may just want a few more moments to consider all the facts and figures you're providing. Handled properly, minor objections tend to fade away and your presentation can continue.

A major objection is something you cannot overcome. For example, if your prospect just doesn't have enough money to make the purchase or option for getting the money elsewhere, it's impossible for him or her to become a client.

When you encounter a major objection (and it truly is a major objection), it's time to disengage. Be courteous. Don't brush off the buyer, but at this point it's time to move on so you can help the people who can actually purchase your product. In other words, if there's no way to win this game, don't play this round.

Key #4: Never argue. This creates an impossible situation. As a trained presenter, the salesperson usually has the edge and can win the argument. This leaves the buyer with only one vehicle for getting even for the shabby and unprofessional way he or she has been treated. You guessed it, buying from somebody else. It's called "payback" and in that situation, everybody except the competition loses.

Key #5: Keep the potential client separate from the objection. Objections are necessary feedback to tell you where you need to direct your presentation. It's very easy to "hit 'em hard" and in doing so unintentionally "rough up" your buyer. Be sensitive to their feelings. Remember, buying is an emotional process, not a logical one. You can win all the logical battles and still lose the emotional war.

Key #6: Allow your buyer to answer his or her own objections. Never forget that the reason you're talking to this person is because he or she has a need. That's the reason for the visit in the first place. Just ask them questions about their needs and lead them where you want them to go. They'll surprise you every time by providing the answers. Having them provide answers rather than assuming you know their needs is always better because regardless of how ethical and unbiased you may be, in their eyes you still have a vested interest in the sale. If they provide the answer, it just has to be true.

Key #7: Don't interrupt. Avoid the dangerous temptation to jump in and answer the objection right away. Your buyer deserves the right to voice an opinion fully. Besides, the more you let buyers talk, the more likely they'll talk themselves right through the objection or handle it on their own. Maybe they just had to talk it out. Another benefit of letting your potential clients talk is the amount of information you can gain.

Key #8: Feed the objection back. This is especially helpful with couples. One party will object, you feed it back, and the other party will often provide the answer. Try it. It works.

Key #9: Ask for more detail. Be serious about your need for more information and get the buyer talking. This does two things for you: (1) gathers information and (2) gives you time to develop an answer.

Key #10: Provide the answer. Every product or service ever sold has strengths and weaknesses and a champion salesperson has to be ready to discuss those weaknesses honestly and intelligently. Instead of worrying about them or creating nightmare fantasies in your mind, study them. Develop all the different ways you can address the situations. One of the best strategies is to be honest, admit the weakness and then move on to strengths that compensate for it. *"Yes, ma'am, this is an older neighborhood, but you just can't get charm like this in the new subdivisions, plus the homes here have mature trees and excellent resale value."*

Key #11: Make sure the buyer understands your answer. The simplest way to do this is just to ask.

"Doesn't that clarify the answer for you?"

"Now that we've answered that question, we can go ahead, can't we?"

"That solves your concern with _____, doesn't it?"

One of the worst things you can do in a presentation is to leave an objection out there unanswered. It's like a land mine just waiting for your step to blow up the sales opportunity.

Key #12: Move on! Once you've answered the objection and confirmed that it has been understood, move on to the next step in your presentation.

Key #13: Allow the buyer to see things from your perspective. This is especially effective when someone offers a direct and forceful objection. *"I've tried your product. I don't like it."* Ask the buyer to imagine being the president of your company (or sales manager, etc.) and ask, *"What would you do in his/her position?"* The answer will come back swift and hard. *"I'd do this, that and the other."* At that point you note that *"this, that and the other"* is very likely what your president did to solve the issue (if that's truly what was done). This is the old *"walk a mile in another man's moccasins"* technique except you're allowing the buyer to put on the shoe leather.

Key #14: *"Thanks. We appreciate your time. We'll get back to you"* usually means we're headed out to find the same thing, only cheaper. Answer this by a technique we call questioning down. Ask for permission to ask a few questions before they leave and then run through the positives of your product or service. *"We've agreed that this meets your quality standards... and it's the right size...and you're impressed with our service after the sale policy..."* and so on. Eventually, you'll get them to admit the real objection is the investment, which is good. Once you've identified that as the key concern, you can begin to address it.

Key #15: If there are no major objections and the buyer doesn't go ahead with the purchase, accept your responsibility for the lost sale. The next step is to learn from all your mistakes, study up on the techniques and strategies you need to use more effectively, and move on to the next sale. *"It's my fault"* is a necessary step toward professional growth, one that leads directly to *"It's my sale!"*

Conclusion

In the introduction to *Sell It Today, Sell It Now*™, *Mastering the Art of the One-Call Close*, we stressed the importance of using a proper sequence in the sales process. We followed this thought throughout the book, from the job description to the mind of the salesperson on through to the mind of the consumer and beyond. We promised something else in the introduction, that we'd show you how important proper sequence is in every aspect of life, as well.

If you were to ask most people to name the top two professions in terms of stature in the mindset of the American culture, you would most certainly get the same answers pretty much across the board: medicine and law. Yes, both professions have taken a lot of public relations hits. However, we're pretty sure that most parents would be as proud as they could be to have a doctor or an attorney in the family.

How many parents do you think would list the profession of sales? Hopefully, you would.

All three professions have dramatic effects on the people they touch. And of the three, salespeople touch more people in more places in more ways and more times than the other two.

In medicine and law, the aspiring professional doesn't have the option of changing the "sequence" that must occur before he or she can hang out that professional shingle. For example, in medicine, the future doctor must not only get good marks in high school and college, he or she must then enter a long training program that includes Pre-Med, Medical School, Internship and Residency. And that's before they can even begin their careers.

Prospective lawyers must complete a similar sequence of challenges before emerging as the next Clarence Darrow or technical advisor to *Law & Order* or the latest John Grisham film.

By the way, because these professions have such an impact on the individuals, corporations, and organizations they serve, these sequences are mandated by law. The good news, and sometimes the bad news, is that the person choosing the profession of sales is not required to endure such a rigorous regimen (sequence) to enter the field.

We agree that doctors and lawyers, who frequently are engaged in life-or-death matters, may face a more urgent set of circumstances than most salespeople. We do, however, believe that this fact doesn't lessen the responsibility of the salesperson to become as professional as possible.

Unfortunately, for the aspiring sales professional, the sequence of becoming a success in the sales profession can be a rather unstructured one. You're pretty much left to your own devices. Of course, companies provide product knowledge and perhaps some rudimentary training and there are always classes and seminars. But how many universities offer a degree in selling? The answer: Very few.

Reflect on this. Did you stay up late nights during school studying and memorizing math, history, a foreign language, etc. to please your parents or get to the next grade? We are pretty sure you'll answer "yes." You invested time and effort and *"burned the midnight oil"* to avoid getting an F, right?

Now answer this question. Is your knowledge of math, history, or a foreign language helping you earn much of a living today? We are just as sure that the answer to that question is a clear and concise *"No, not as much as I thought it would."* We're finishing these questions for you because we want to put something in perspective.

If you study the book you are holding with the same diligence you studied in school; if you impress upon yourself the importance of avoiding failure in sales; if you'll put forward that same effort; this book will not only make you a tremendous amount of money, it will make you a true professional, and a master of the art of the one-call close.

It is our hope that by reading this book, you will be better prepared to be a sales professional, a real champion; that by following the sequences provided in these pages, your antici-pated sequence of your sales career will be enhanced, and that it will have an on-going, positive impact on your clients, your company, your community, your family, and, yes, yourself.

Together, we wish you greatness!

Increase Your Selling Skills with Additional Training by Tom Hopkins

Books

How to Master the Art of Selling

The Official Guide to Success

Mastering the Art of Selling Real Estate

Low Profile Selling

Selling for Dummies

The Certifiable Salesperson with Laura Laaman

Laugh Your Way to Health & Wealth

How to Master the Art of Selling Financial Services

Selling in Tough Times

When Buyers Say No with Ben Katt

Audio CDs

How to Master the Art of Selling Anything

Achieving Sales Excellence

Low Profile Selling

The Official Guide to Success

Balance Your Life

Academy of Master Closing

Back to the Future in Sales with J. Douglas Edwards

A Collection of Timeless Training

How to Make Your Dreams Come True (for children)

Mastering the Art of Listing Real Estate

Mastering the Art of Selling Real Estate

Tom Hopkins LIVE – Developing Real Estate Champions

How to Master the Art of Selling Financial Services

MP3s

Sell It Today, Sell It Now – Mastering the Art of the One-Call close

How to Master the Art of Selling Anything

Achieving Sales Excellence

Low Profile Selling

The Official Guide to Success

Balance Your Life

Academy of Master Closing

Back to the Future in Sales with J. Douglas Edwards

A Collection of Timeless Training

How to Make Your Dreams Come True (for children)

Mastering the Art of Listing Real Estate

Mastering the Art of Selling Real Estate

Tom Hopkins LIVE – Developing Real Estate Champions

How to Master the Art of Selling Financial Services

Powerful Communication Skills MP3

10 Biggest Sales & Marketing Mistakes and How to Avoid Them MP3

Building Lifetime Clients Through Effective Customer Services MP3

The ABCs of a Successful Career MP3

A Day in the Life of a Million Dollar Producer MP3 (real estate)

Mastering the Art of Mortgage Sales MP3

How to Gain, Train, and Maintain an Effective Sales Force MP3

J. Douglas Edwards' Foundations of Modern Selling MP3

DVDs

Attitude is Everything

Motivate Your Mind

Highlights of the Perfect Sales Process

Closing the Sale

Tom's Worst Day in Sales

Sell It Today, Sell It Now – Mastering the Art of the One-Call Close

Practice, Drill and Rehears for Top Performance

Turning Internet Leads into Sales Dollars

Working with Short Sales & Foreclosures

Qualifying Your Way to Faster Sales (financial services)

Building Sales Champions (DVD system – 12 sessions)

Developing Real Estate Champions (DVD system – 7 sessions)

All of these training materials can be found at www.tom-hopkins.com/training.

CPSIA information can be obtained at www.ICGtesting.com
Printed in the USA
BVOW01s1332180916

462508BV00001B/32/P